Learning
Stories

Education at SAGE

SAGE is a leading international publisher of journals, books, and electronic media for academic, educational, and professional markets.

Our education publishing includes:

- accessible and comprehensive texts for aspiring education professionals and practitioners looking to further their careers through continuing professional development

- inspirational advice and guidance for the classroom

- authoritative state of the art reference from the leading authors in the field

Find out more at: **www.sagepub.co.uk/education**

Learning Stories

Constructing Learner Identities in Early Education

Margaret Carr
and
Wendy Lee

Los Angeles | London | New Delhi
Singapore | Washington DC

First published 2012

Reprinted 2012, 2013, 2017

SAGE Publications Ltd
1 Oliver's Yard
55 City Road
London EC1Y 1SP

SAGE Publications Inc.
2455 Teller Road
Thousand Oaks, California 91320

SAGE Publications India Pvt Ltd
B 1/I 1 Mohan Cooperative Industrial Area
Mathura Road
New Delhi 110 044

SAGE Publications Asia-Pacific Pte Ltd
3 Church Street
#10-04 Samsung Hub
Singapore 049483

Library of Congress Control Number: 2011929638

British Library Cataloguing in Publication data

A catalogue record for this book is available from the British Library

ISBN 978-0-85702-092-5
ISBN 978-0-85702-093-2 (pbk)

Typeset by C&M Digitals (P) Ltd, Chennai, India
Printed in Great Britain by Ashford Colour Press Ltd

To our parents, grandparents and great grandparents, whose lives taught us about courage and resilience and who bequeathed us some good stories.

Contents

List of Learning Stories

List of Tables

About the Authors

Margaret Carr is a Professor of Education at the Wilf Malcolm Institute of Educational Research at the University of Waikato, New Zealand. She was a Co-Director of the New Zealand Early Childhood Curriculum Development project that developed the national curriculum, Te Whāriki, published in 1996. After Te Whāriki was published, she researched in five different early childhood settings – a childcare centre, a kindergarten, a playcentre, a kōhanga reo (Māori language immersion early childhood centre) and a home-based setting to develop, with the teachers, Learning Stories as a narrative assessment practice that was aligned with the sociocultural focus of Te Whāriki. Since then she has researched and published widely on issues of curriculum and assessment in the early years. Formerly a kindergarten teacher, Margaret has taught student teachers in the undergraduate and graduate teacher education programme at the Faculty of Education, and she has a great enthusiasm for co-researching with teachers on action research projects, where the topics are dilemmas and puzzles about curriculum development and assessment that interest the teachers.

Wendy Lee is the Director of the Educational Leadership Project (Ltd), a professional learning provider for the early childhood sector in New Zealand. Wendy has been involved in the Early Childhood Education (ECE) field as a teacher, tutor, lecturer, manager, professional development facilitator and researcher. She has collaborated on three research projects in early years settings with Margaret Carr: *question-asking and question-exploring*, *learning wisdom* and *learning in the making: disposition and design in early education*. Prior to this she was a Co-Director with Margaret of the National Early Childhood Assessment and Learning Exemplar Project that developed the *Kei Tua o te Pae* books on assessment for learning in early childhood for the New Zealand early childhood sector. Wendy has a deep interest in curriculum and leadership issues for ECE. She has presented at conferences on early childhood curriculum, leadership and Learning Stories throughout the world, including the UK, Germany, Japan, Iceland, Belgium, the USA, the United Arab Emirates, Norway, the Czech Republic, Canada, Australia and Sweden.

Preface and Acknowledgements

This book is about the role of documentation and assessment in the construction of learner identities in the early years. It discusses the purposes and the consequences of a narrative assessment practice, Learning Stories, that was developed in a country where the early childhood curriculum, Te Whāriki, had emphasised learning as responsive and reciprocal relationships with people, places and things. *Learning Stories: Constructing Learner Identities in Early Education* follows the 2001 *Assessment in Early Childhood Settings: Learning Stories*, published by Paul Chapman which was then the education arm of SAGE Publications. In the decade since the 2001 book, there has been much innovative development work on Learning Stories, often during collaborations between professional development facilitators and teachers, as well as between university academics and teachers in action or practitioner research projects and programmes. Wendy had led professional development projects as Director of the Educational Leadership Project (ELP), Margaret had explored these ideas with university students, and both of us have worked together on a number of research projects with teachers. It seemed to be the right time to recognise this work in a new book.

We acknowledge here the Ministry of Education in New Zealand for the professional development programme and practitioner research opportunities during this time. Both of us have been centrally involved with projects in the *Centres of Innovation* programme from 2003 to 2009 (Meade, 2005, 2006, 2007, 2010), the writing of the 20 books in the *Kei Tua o te Pae Assessment for Learning: Early Childhood Exemplars* resource from 2004 to 2009, the professional development that supported that resource from 2006 to 2010, and the Teaching and Learning Research Initiative (TLRI) programme, funded by the Ministry and administered so effectively by the New Zealand Council for Educational Research. The TLRI programme has emphasised research in partnership with practitioners and research that makes a difference for teachers, families and learners. Working on the *Kei tua o te pae* books had taught us that the triad of theory, research evidence and examples is valuable for a range of audiences. So planning for this co-authored book began.

A number of research projects with teachers have provided examples, case studies, conversations and reflections for this book. These projects have various titles and intentions: *Learning Wisdom* in nine early childhood centres; *A Question-asking and Question-exploring Culture* in a childcare centre; *Transition to School* in a kindergarten; *Integrating ICTs with Teaching and Learning in the Early Years* in a kindergarten; *Te Tamaiti hei Raukura* (later *Te Pito Mata*) in a kōhanga reo (Māori immersion language nest); *Key Learning Competencies across Place and Time* in three schools and two childcare centres; and *Strengthening Responsive and Reciprocal Relationships in a Whānau Tangata Centre* in a kindergarten. A Royal Society of New Zealand Marsden

Fund project was published as *Learning in the Making: Disposition and Design in the Early Years* and some of the findings in that project have been included here as well. We acknowledge with respect and affection the other Research Associates and collaborative partners on these projects: Jeanette Clarkin-Phillips, Keryn Davis, Judith Duncan, Carolyn Jones, Kate Marshall, Te Wharehuia Milroy, Sue Molloy, Sally Peters, Anne B. Smith and Tina Williams. The ELP team acted as facilitators in the *Learning Wisdom* project: Alison Brierley, Jo Colbert, Kathryn Delany, Julie Killick, Robyn Lawrence, Lorraine Sands and Helen Sola-Nanai.

The term 'practitioner inquiry' has been used to refer to 'the array of educational research genres where the practitioner is the researcher, the professional context is the research site, and practice itself is the focus of study' (Cochran-Smith and Donnell, 2006: 503). Our experience tells us that practitioner inquiry has the capacity to construct theory and to contribute to an understanding of knowing and learning that goes beyond the local, informing the everyday practice in other places. This notion of practitioner research has been embedded in the Educational Leadership Project programme (www.elp. co.nz) since 2000. In all of these practitioner projects teachers and research associates collaboratively developed ideas that made a difference to their own reflections on practice and to their pedagogy, while at the same time they have contributed to our thinking and to the writing of this book. We acknowledge with gratitude the contributions from the children's families and teachers in these projects. The schools and early childhood settings are acknowledged on p. xv. The Learning Stories in the book illustrate or exemplify a point being made: they were not chosen because they are exemplary or 'perfect'. They come from particular contexts and not much information about their learners or their environments and communities is included in them, so they should be read as contributing to the debate and critique that should accompany discussions about assessment. We hope that readers will re-contextualise the messages that the examples and the attached text tell.

We were especially delighted when SAGE agreed that a substantial number of the examples could be in full colour. We hoped that this opportunity to include so many authentic examples would make the book interesting to teachers and student teachers, and that the research and theoretical ideas underpinning the notion of narrative assessments would also be interesting to the academy. As in the earlier book, we have sought an alignment of practice and theory. It has been a complex jigsaw to put together – including Learning Story examples, case studies of teachers' interactions with children, quotes from theoretical writers, and comments from teachers. We have greatly appreciated the tolerance, trust and competence of the SAGE team: Jude Bowen, who had the idea of a new book, Alex Molineux, Thea Watson, copy-editor Roza El-Eini, proofreader Christine Bitten and indexer Bill Farrington who have worked with us to design and construct this mosaic of ideas and examples. Thanks too to Malcom Carr and Kathleen Ullal for careful editing at the New Zealand end.

The earlier book often foregrounded the children; in this book we have included many more teachers' voices. Quotes from teachers begin each chapter – except for Chapter 4, where a parent comment opens the discussion. This 'second generation' of Learning Story teachers have been making the most of the possibilities of new digital technologies, writing the assessments with and for the learners as well as for the families, revisiting the portfolios with children, talking with them about their learning, and puzzling with their co-teachers over the analysis of learning outcomes.

The first Learning Stories book had looked closely at one of the more neglected of assessed outcomes in early childhood discussions, learning dispositions, because these had been introduced in the 1996 national early childhood curriculum, Te Whāriki. This book widens the lense to explore learner outcomes as a mingling and merging of stores of knowledge with stores of disposition, inviting 'spilt-screen' or dual focus pedagogies (Claxton, Chambers, Powell and Lucas, 2011) and assessments. It describes (in Chapter 1, for instance) the classroom assessment work of teachers like Yvonne S. who constructs portfolios and Learning Stories in which reporting on numeracy, literacy, science, art – and so on – is closely woven into and with stories of learning episodes that also take note of the dispositions and possible selves that accompanied the learning. By 2007 a new school curriculum in New Zealand had introduced dispositional outcomes – *key competencies*. In that school curriculum document an alignment was described across the sectors: the school key competencies were aligned with the strands of outcome in Te Whā riki. Table 5.1 in Chapter 5 includes that alignment, together with some of the longer term dispositional processes highlighted in teachers' work. School classroom teachers, together with their principals, have been exploring the inclusion of key competencies in their pedagogy in many imaginative ways, including using Learning Stories in their assessments, and we have included a number of these. Four of these stories (from Michael, Molly, Leilani and Bayley), and the quotes from Gary and Raymond in Chapter 7, were originally collected in Christchurch in 2010 and 2011 for a DVD resource on Learning Stories in schools to be published by NZCER Press at the same time as this book. Our thanks to NZCER Press for permission to include them here. We acknowledge the assistance of Keryn Davis and Jocelyn Wright in enabling us to access this work during the very difficult time following the devastating Christchurch earthquakes of September 2010 and February 2011, and we take this opportunity to salute the resilience of these facilitators, teachers, children and families in this earthquake-torn city.

Questions of resilience and democracy have been in our minds as we have worked in early childhood, and as we were writing this book. Contested terrain is traversed here, as Michel Vandenbroeck and Maria Bouverne-De Bie (2006: 128) indicated when they examined how the 'concepts of participation, children's rights and "agency" may be troubled as discursive regimes'. They argued that it seems necessary to integrate both 'macro' (the broader social structure) and 'micro' (positioning children in their own contexts) approaches to these concepts. We have in this book zoomed in on examples at the 'micro' level, often analysing them for their 'middle-level situated meanings' (Gee, 1997, 2000–2001). At a 'macro' level, this book is written at a time of globalisation and globalised crises where the response from many is to hunker down and look after the individual and the short-term. In a paper entitled 'Education for democracy: reasons and strategies', Wolfgang Edelstein comments that, across the world, there are now 'serious threats to the very foundations and basic components of democratic systems: the corrosion, as Münkler calls it, of the *sociomoral resources of democracy*' (italics in the original). He adds, and we agree, that:

> A democratic school is not a luxury. Learning democracy is not just an extension of the serious business of learning for life. It is the serious business of learning for life and, as such, it must be a central goal of education in school. (Edelstein, 2011: 127)

The requirements for learning democracy, the 'non-cognitive' and difficult-to-measure skills and dispositions towards kindness and responsibility and dialogue, as well as agency, emotional development, curiosity and the resilience to persevere with difficult tasks, can be fostered in the early years. They contribute in the longer term to the growth of well-being and the culture of the community at large. At the same time, the obverse is true: individualistic, undemocratic and disempowering environments and purposes in the early years can contribute towards the development of these qualities in adulthood. Assessment in the early years contributes centrally to this learning, and, although it is a complex task to assess them, we ignore these dispositions at our peril. Gunilla Dahlberg and Peter Moss (2005: vi) warn that the 'increasing institutionalisation of childhood may lead to greater and more effective governing of children' and they point out that this may happen if early childhood institutions are understood as 'enclosures for the effective application of technologies to produce predetermined and standardised outcomes'. This book suggests some alternative possibilities: early childhood practitioners constructed not as technicians, but as ethical and thoughtful theorists and commentators as well as caring and competent teachers; learning outcomes as dispositional and relational, sited in 'the middle' between the learner and the particular cultural environment; a major educational outcome as the appropriation of a repertoire of learner identities and possible selves; and learning described as inextricably distributed across the child, the family and community, the teachers, and the cultural resources available. The possibilities for an assessment practice to connect all this together in educational places of interpretation, personalisation, wise practice, dialogue and joy are the major discussion points in this book.

We acknowledge with gratitude the Learning Stories, transcripts, case studies, and research project conversations that contributed to our thinking about Learning Stories from teachers at the following early childhood centres and schools.

Aratupu Preschool and Nursery

Awhi Whanau Early Childhood Centre

Carol White Family and Children's Centre

Discovery 1 School

Faamasani Aoga Amata Preschool

Flat Bush Kindergarten

Greerton Early Childhood Centre

Halswell Primary School

Harbourview Kindergarten

Highland Park Kindergarten

Hinemoa Kindergarten

Hornby Primary School

Hungerford Nursery School Centre for Children and Families, Berkshire, England

Kids Express

Kita Sommergarten, Berlin, Germany

Lady Gowrie Childcare Centre, Adelaide, South Australia

St Paulinus Primary School, Guisborough, England

Tai Tamariki Kindergarten

Taitoko Kindergarten

Te Kōhanga Reo o Mana Tamariki

Mangere Bridge Kindergarten

Mangere Bridge Primary School

New Brighton Community Preschool and Nursery

Northcote Primary School

Otahuhu Kindergarten

Pakuranga Baptist Kindergarten

Papanui Primary School

Papatoetoe Kindergarten

Parkview Primary School

Pigeon Mountain Kindergarten

Roskill South Kindergarten

Rotorua Primary School

Stanmore Bay Kindergarten

York House Nursery, Durham, England

1

Learner Identities in Early Education: An Introduction to Four Themes

Box 1.1

In the Learning Story *Design Inspiration* we can see Kyah's willingness to be flexible with the goals she sets herself. Kyah could see that the picture [in a book] of wearable art was made up of old pairs of jeans and recognised that in order to make her own rendition she was not going to be able to use the same materials as the original artist but instead had to make alternative choices with the resources that she had available to her. ... Kyah's view of herself as a learner comes directly from her family's and her teachers' attitudes to learning and intelligence. A paper entitled *Learning is Learnable* (Claxton, 2004: 3) documents how much people unintentionally '*pick up*' not just their physical but mental habits and values from those around them. We are deeply immersed in a community of learners, and teachers have a vital role, particularly for children who spend large parts of their days in an early learning, group setting. (Karen H., early childhood teacher, commenting on a Learning Story during a research project)

This quote from a teacher, writing about an episode of learning for 4-year-old Kyah, introduces four themes about the ways that Kyah views herself as a learner. These themes are about young learners who construct their own opportunities to learn, make learning connections from one place to another, recognise the learning journey that they are on, and explore their understandings in a range of increasingly complex ways.

This book will also consider these themes as *consequences for assessment practice.* Assessment for learning plays a powerful role in this early construction of a learner identity. It is the Learning Story and its portfolio – revisited with others – that enables Kyah to recognise the learning journey that is valued here. We are particularly interested in the role of narrative assessments: adults and children telling and re-telling stories of learning and competence, reflecting on the past and planning for the future. As Kyah's teacher points out, significant numbers of young people now spend substantial periods of time each week in early years education group settings – early childhood and school. So we must pay close attention to these themes and consequences.

The teacher's comment at the beginning of this chapter highlights the way in which the valued adults in Kyah's life view learning and how this makes a difference to Kyah's view of herself as a learner. It also points out that early childhood settings and families can be described as 'communities of learners' in which habits and values to do with learning (as well as many other domains of life) are intentionally, and unintentionally, 'picked up' by participants. Pierre Bourdieu (1990) has had much to say about this, arguing that these values and ways of being are handed down from generation to generation as *habitus*: 'systems of durable, transposable dispositions' that inscribe 'things to do or not to do, things to say or not to say, in relation to a "probable" upcoming future' (p. 53). In the twenty-first century this intergenerational or *vertical* development has become complicated by the growth of early childhood provision and by the international migration of people and ideas. Learning communities extend across the globe now, and the World Wide Web and its social and information networking has a powerful influence on our views about a 'probable' upcoming future. One of our responses to this is to argue that we must now, as well, do more to strengthen the *horizontal* and intersecting circles of influence on learner identity in early childhood provision: connecting the cultures' values, goals and visions across early years educational communities – families, early childhood settings outside the home and schools. Martin Packer and David Greco-Brooks (1999) are two of many writers who have argued that school classrooms are not just places where knowledge and skills are taught (an *epistemological* project); they include *ontological work* (p. 135). Ontological work includes the construction and editing of learner identities and the offering of new possibilities for durable, relocatable dispositions that inscribe things to do or not to do, things to say or not to say and our expectations for the future.

This is true, too, of any places that provide early childhood care and education outside the home. Analysing narratives of three recently arrived immigrant mothers attending child care centres in Belgium during the weeks prior to their young children's entry to school, Michel Vandenbroeck, Griet Roets and Aïsji Snoeck (2009) have commented that 'the child care centre may be considered as a place where a shared repertoire of cultural patterns is constructed and jointly reconfigured' (p. 209) and one that can challenge the idea of fixed national identities and unitary selves. They acknowledge the writing of Rosi Braidotti (1994) to refer to 'the nomadic subject' (p. 158), 'a hybrid and interconnected identity that occupies a variety of possible subject positions' (Vandenbroeck et al., 2009: 211). Kyah's story, too, implies at least two possible subject positions: a learner who improvises and a fabric designer. Jenelle, a teacher at this centre, had written a Learning Story

about Kyah's design work on this occasion. The centre had been given a book on 'wearable art' from a recent exhibition, and one of the designs was created using 10 metres of denim: it looked like a ball gown made out of children's denim jeans. Kyah constructed her own version, bringing some old clothes from home.

Many of the ideas in this book are encapsulated in the following quote from Jerome Bruner (2002):

> It is through narrative that we create and re-create selfhood, and self is a product of our telling and re-telling. We are, from the start, expressions of our culture. Culture is replete with alternative narratives about what self is or might be. (p. 86)

The notion that culture is replete with 'alternative narratives about what self is or might be' is exactly the place where we would like this book to be heading: that children develop repertoires of shared cultural patterns and valued possible learner selves, a product, in part, of learning-story telling and retelling. We argue that teachers, children and families can become co-authors of this telling and re-telling, and that these repertoires are made up of a complex intermingling of stores of knowledge with stores of disposition.

We highlight the teachers' views here, and we have long admired the ways in which teachers of young children are prepared to struggle with and puzzle over the dilemmas and the tensions of the profession. Perhaps because the impetus for much of our thinking has been our work with teachers implementing a bicultural and bilingual curriculum, our ideas resonate with the notion of learning as a cultural process. A chapter in the *Handbook of the learning sciences* by Na'ilah Suad Nasir, Ann Rosebery, Beth Warren and Carol Lee (2006) entitled 'Learning as a cultural process: Achieving equity through diversity' discusses the ways in which culture is central to learning:

> By 'culture', we mean the constellation of practices historically developed and dynamically shaped by communities in order to accomplish the purposes they value. Such practices are constituted by the tools they use, the social networks with which they are connected, the ways they organize joint activity, the discourses they use and value (i.e., specific ways of conceptualizing, representing, evaluating and engaging with the world). On this view, learning and development can be seen as the acquisition throughout the life course of diverse repertoires of overlapping, complementary, or even conflicting cultural practices. (p. 489)

Our aim in the book is to explore the contribution that narrative assessment as Learning Stories can make towards the construction of a repertoire of cultural practices and learner identities. Our perspective on learner identity and this construction process centrally includes: agency and dialogue (the ways in which joint activity is organised), making connections across boundaries between places (the social networks with which the practice is connected), recognising and re-cognising learning continuities, and appropriating knowledges and learning dispositions in a range of increasingly complex ways (the discourses that are used and valued). Nasir et al. (2006) wrote that cultural practices are constituted, in part, by the tools that communities use. The tools that we will primarily focus on here are the assessment practices, and we will conclude that the tools that assess the learning can also sustain the learning by influencing the other parts of the cultural constellation – the social networks, the way that 'joint activity' is organised and the discourses that are used and valued.

Agency and Dialogue

In Karen's account of Kyah's sense of self that introduced this chapter she comments on the role of 'her family's and her teachers' attitudes to learning and intelligence'. Kyah is positioned in the early childhood centre as a powerful learner, a participant with agency, someone who is disposed to take on an authoring role. Karen was reminded of Guy Claxton's insistence that 'learning is learnable' (Claxton, 2004) and James Greeno (2006) has argued that learning will be more likely to be sustained if learners are positioned as authoritative and accountable. Finding opportunities for this can be a challenge for teachers. In Iram Siraj-Blatchford's (2010: 157) discussion of case studies of effective practice from the longitudinal Effective Provision of Preschool Education (EPPE) project in England she comments that the 'excellent' settings were found to encourage 'sustained shared thinking'. She describes sustained shared thinking as 'any episode in which two or more individuals "worked together" in an intellectual way to solve a problem, clarify a concept, evaluate activities, extend a narrative etc.', and she added that 'The research found that this did not happen very frequently'.

Genuine dialogue requires the deliberate creation of opportunity for initiative-sharing and collaboration, and, as Urie Bronfenbrenner's (1979) commentary on social roles as contexts of human development suggests:

> The greater the degree of power socially sanctioned for a given role, the greater the tendency for the role occupant to exercise and exploit the power and for those in a subordinate position to respond by increased submission, dependency, and lack of initiative. (p. 92)

Here is Naomi, a teacher who has been revisiting the stories of their learning with three- and four-year-old children, reflecting on the quality of her conversations with Rose:

> I have instigated many of these revisiting conversations and sometimes I have not chosen my timing well and the conversation has reflected this; the child doesn't seem too interested and so I am having to lead the discussion; this often leads to my asking too many questions and the child does not say much. Today my timing was different in that I could see Rose was looking for someone to share her portfolio with and I seized the moment, offering to be that person for her. What a difference between this conversation and the first one I initiated with Rose. For the most part she led the conversation and I followed; I think this shows in comparing the length of my first conversation with Rose [18 verbal turns] and this one [six weeks later: 74 verbal turns]. (Naomi, teacher)

Naomi comments that 'for the most part she led the conversation and I followed'; this describes a dialogue in which Rose has a degree of power or agency.

Learning 'in the Middle'

The references to 'self' in the quote from Jerome Bruner earlier in this chapter, and elsewhere in this chapter to 'identities' and to 'possible selves' provide a glimpse into the contested theoretical territory inhabited by 'selves', 'identities', possible selves and 'subject positions'. We have settled on 'identity', a common word in the sociocultural literature. There is a strong resonance between Nasir's view of learning as a cultural process and James Gee's sociocultural notion of a Discourse, interesting to us here because he goes on to write about 'a sociocultural perspective on opportunities to learn' in a book about assessment. Gee (2008) compares a traditional view with a *situated/sociocultural* viewpoint:

> A situated/sociocultural viewpoint looks at knowledge and learning not primarily in terms of representation in the head, although there is no need to deny that such representations exist and play an important role. Rather, it looks at knowledge and learning in terms of a *relationship* between an individual with both a mind and a body and an environment in which the individual thinks, feels and interacts. Both the body and the environment tend to be backgrounded in traditional views of knowledge and learning. (p. 81)

The term 'sociocultural' is also used by James Wertsch (1991) because, he writes, he wanted to 'understand how mental action is situated in cultural, historical and institutional settings' (p. 15). His ideas will contribute to this chapter in other ways as well. He writes that, rather than speaking of 'individual(s)', he prefers to speak of 'individual(s)-acting-with-mediational-means' (p. 12). He later writes (1998: 65) that 'a focus on mediated action and the cultural tools employed in it makes it possible to "live in the middle" and to address the cultural situatedness of action, power and authority'. Guiding our analysis, too, is the view that a learning activity is distributed over social and cultural practices; Peggy Miller and Jacqueline Goodnow (1995) say that the learner is a 'person-participating-in-a-practice' (p. 8). We are interested in what goes on in this space 'in the middle', in the reciprocal relationship between an educational environment and the learning individual. Assessment sits in this space, so these discussions by James Gee, James Wertsch, Peggy Miller and Jacqueline Goodnow have been helpful.

Ideas about agency and identity have influenced curriculum documents in the South Pacific. The 2009 Early Years Framework for Australia is entitled, 'Belonging, Being and Becoming' (Commonwealth of Australia, 2009). One of the five Learning Outcomes is a 'strong sense of identity' and three other outcomes are about connection, involvement and communication: children are connected with and contribute to their world; children are confident and involved learners; children are effective communicators. These outcomes are *learning in the middle*. The other Learning Outcome in this Framework is 'children have a strong sense of well-being'. In this document a strong sense of well-being includes confidence and optimism, a 'sense of agency and a desire to interact with responsive others' (p. 30). The foundation curriculum document for Learning Stories was the New Zealand national early childhood curriculum document, Te Whāriki, with its five strands of integrated knowledges and dispositional outcomes (Ministry of Education, 1996). In Māori these strands are: mana tangata, mana atua, mana aotūroa, mana reo, mana whenua. There is no easy translation into English of *mana*: it is about authority, prestige, empowerment. The Māori curriculum strands are domains of *mana*, and might be described as five sources of authority and empowerment: people; spiritual, mental and physical well-being; knowledge of the world in the widest sense; language; and place. The English equivalents (but not direct translations) in the curriculum document are: contribution, well-being, exploration, communication and belonging.[2]

Writing that the formation of identities in education includes students needing 'ways of having an effect on the world and making their actions matter' Etienne Wenger (1998) elaborates:

Talking about learning in terms of these modes of belonging makes it possible to consider educational designs not just in terms of the delivery of a curriculum, but more generally in terms of their effects on the formation of identities. Students need:

1 places of engagement
2 materials and experiences with which to build an image of the world and themselves
3 ways of having an effect on the world and making their actions matter. (p. 270)

Peter Johnston (2004) writes that 'the spark of agency is simply the perception that the environment is responsive to our actions' (p. 9). Kyah's teacher, in her commentary, has described just such a place, or community, of engagement in which Kyah's actions are deemed to matter and are documented because they are important.

Making Connections Across Boundaries Between Places

The second foundational idea in this book is that children's capability to recognise opportunity and to use their learning in new contexts is enhanced if there is communication about their education between the home and school or early childhood setting. Writing about identity again, Wenger (1998) has also commented that coordinating multiple perspectives 'is one of the most critical aspects of education for the kind of world we live in', and that this is a matter of 'straddling across boundaries':

To be able to have effects on the world, students must learn to find ways of coordinating multiple perspectives. This observation is rather commonplace. What is not so widely understood is that this ability is not just a matter of information and skill. It is not an abstract technical question, not merely learning the repertoire of multiple practices. Rather, it is a matter of identity – of straddling across boundaries and finding ways of being in the world that can encompass multiple, conflicting perspectives in the course of addressing significant issues. Exercising this sort of identity is a result of participation in a learning community challenged by issues of alignment. It is one of the most critical aspects of education for the kind of world we live in. (p. 274)

Family Expectations

Different expectations in intersecting places is one aspect of this alignment. A synthesis of over 800 meta-analyses relating to educational achievement by John Hattie (2009) found that parental expectations are far more powerful than many of the structural features of the home (single or two-parent families, families with resident or non-resident fathers, divorced parents, adopted or non-adopted children, or only children and non-only children):

> Parents have major effects in terms of the encouragement and expectations that they transmit to their children. Many parents, however, struggle to comprehend the language of learning and thus are disadvantaged in the methods they use to encourage their children to attain their expectations. Across all home variables, parental aspirations and expectations for children's educational achievement has the strongest relationship with achievement. (p. 70)

The research in England by Liz Brooker (2002) has provided powerful examples of parents who struggled to comprehend the language of learning. Andrew Pollard and Ann Filer's (Pollard and Filer, 1999; Filer and Pollard, 2000) research on patterns of learning orientation concluded that parents of young children played a significant role in discussing, mediating and interpreting school experiences and new challenges.

In one of our studies, we traced the development over 18 months from early childhood into school for Ofeina. Her mother, the fifth of seven children, had migrated to New Zealand from Tonga when she was a teenager and when she left school she held down two jobs for a number of years to help support the family. Ofeina, her older brother and a cousin were looked after by their grandmother during the day and after preschool and school, while their parents worked. The grandmother spoke mostly in Tongan to the children, and both Tongan and English were spoken in Ofeina's home. Here is Ofeina's mother talking about her ambitions for her children:

> I told them, you go to University, 'cos I didn't, I know I should have but I didn't. I worked part-time when I was at school; when I was (in the) sixth form I had to get a part-time job to help out ... I keep saying to my son 'even if they say you can't, you have to do your best'. (Carr, Smith, Duncan, Jones, Lee and Marshall, 2010: 63–72)

Ofeina, at age five, knew that this was a possible future for her.

Assessments as Boundary Objects

A number of researchers, in a range of contexts, write about the role of *boundary* objects in the coordinating of multiple and conflicting viewpoints. Susan Star and James Griesemer (1989) conclude that, 'The creation and management of boundary objects is a key process in developing and maintaining coherence across intersecting social worlds' (p. 393). Dana Walker and Honorine Nocon (2007) researched a 'hip-hop' dance activity in an after-school programme and described boundary-crossing competence as 'the ability to function competently in multiple contexts'. They write about 'recontextualisation' and 'boundary processes that involve cultural brokers and boundary objects' (p. 179). Writing about assessments, and acknowledging this earlier work on boundary objects, Pamela Moss, Brian Girard and James Greeno (2008) include documented assessments as boundary objects. They comment that the concept of 'boundary object':

> provides additional theoretical resources for the analysis of documentary assessments. A boundary object is an object that inhabits multiple heterogeneous social worlds [or activity systems] and enables communication and cooperation across these worlds. (p. 300, bracketed words in the original)

Learning Stories are boundary objects, with their boundary status and value considerably enhanced when they add another boundary object: the home language. Chapter 4 includes examples of this powerful combination.

Recognising and Re-cognising Learning Continuities

We will be looking closely at the opportunities for children to recognise that they are on a learning journey, and to identify some of the steps along the way. This is the third theme of the book. We will be highlighting learning as a journey and in Chapter 5 we look at Learning Stories as 'chains of learning episodes that bear on some facet of learning or identity development' (Lemke, 2001: 25), but there is a prior requirement for recognising (or re-cognising, changing) continuities, and that is to have an appreciation of the longer-term goal. This goal will be articulated differently in different communities.

Here we introduce the notion of 'possible selves', also introduced in the 2001 Learning Story book (Carr, 2001a: 26). This is an identity description from Hazel Markus and Paula Nurius (1986) that resonates with Bruner's 'alternative narratives about what self is or might be' and Bourdieu's 'things to do or not to do, things to say or not to say, in relation to a "probable" upcoming future'. Markus and Nurius pointed out that 'possible selves derive from representations of the self in the past and they include representations of the self in the future' (p. 954). The 'pool of possible selves derives from the categories made salient by the individual's particular sociocultural and historical context and from the models, images and symbols provided by the media and by the individual's immediate social experiences' (p. 954).

Caroline Gipps (2002), who has written extensively on assessment, has commented on the role of assessment in this. She says:

> Because of the public nature of much questioning and feedback in the classroom, and the power dynamic in the student–teacher relationship, assessment plays a key role in identity formation. The language of assessment and evaluation is one of the routes

by which the social process has to be acknowledged in this sphere: identity is socially bestowed, socially sustained and socially transformed … If identity is conceived as concerned with persuading others and oneself about who one is, and what one is able to do, the judgement of others is crucial. (p. 80)

For Markus and Nurius possible selves are affective-cognitive structures about the self; they 'determine which stimuli are selected for attention' (1986: 955). They can determine what is noticed and recognised. At a primary school using Learning Stories for assessment, for instance, four aims were set out for the school's pupils: resilient learner, thinker, caring citizen, thinker and communicator. These provided cues for analysing the stories of the children's learning.

Robyn G., an early childhood teacher, noticed an episode in which looking at her assessment folder provoked an identity comment from Sela; she recognised it as a significant event.

Box 1.2

I'm a Library Girl

A commentary by Robyn G.

Today I was quietly surrounded by three children. We were revisiting their folders together. Children were exclaiming over the photos of themselves and their friends and recalling what was happening. Sela was leaning on the sofa behind us revisiting her folder alone carefully turning the pages and talking to herself. I was very aware of her and I hadn't seen her show this level of interest in her folder before. She was looking at some photos of herself where she is sitting with one of the school librarians in the school library. Then I heard her say to herself 'I'm a library girl, I'm a library girl' in a sweet sing-songy chant. She said this in a very proud way smiling and to herself. I was astonished as I had never heard Sela speaking in English apart from the odd single word.

I was thrilled to have been so privileged to have had this experience. Going out to the library every week has been an ongoing part of our centre programme for two years now and it is difficult to actually pinpoint children's short-term progress. Sela is now three years old and she had been coming with us for around six months when this happened. She has had first language support from her Burmese teacher Htwe Htwe and I think has a deep understanding and value of her library experience because of this support.

In another example from our research, Kiri, a teacher, is revisiting Andrew's portfolio with him. Andrew asks: 'Is that me doing my book?' (a new Learning Story he hasn't seen about his writing and making a book). Kiri: 'Yes, when you were becoming an author.' Cory, a four-year-old in the same kindergarten, became absorbed by problem-solving experiences with water play and pipes, and Prue, one of the teachers, reflected: 'I was amazed at his concentration for such a long period of time.' Almost a year later she commented on his continued interest in water flow and pipes, as he became more ambitious. She noted in a Learning Story that, 'Further experiments were carried out. Some of them worked and some didn't work so well.' She wrote in the Story: 'This is what happens when we do experiments ... I think scientists make discoveries like this too.' Helen, another teacher, notes in a Learning Story that Kamalpreet is using her portfolio as both a numeracy tool *and* a tool that nurtures her well-being and sense of belonging (see Learning Story 1.1).

Kamalpreet enjoys her portfolio

Term 3 – By Helen
I have noticed that you have become very involved in using your portfolio. At first you used to carry it around a lot with you, and then I started to see you looking at it more often. It has now become a regular thing for you to sit down and read your portfolio to yourself, just as if you were reading a book to yourself. One day, when we were looking at your portfolio together, you paused and counted the pieces of card on your collage picture on one of the pages. I was impressed with your counting skills. I hadn't thought of a portfolio as being a numeracy tool before, so thank you for making me aware of this, Kamalpreet.

What learning am I seeing here:
Kamalpreet, what an amazing sense of ownership you have of your portfolio. For you it is like owning a favourite toy or book that brings you a lot of joy and happiness.

Kamalpreet's interactions with her portfolio appear to nurture her wellbeing and sense of belonging in this kindergarten, her special 'place of play'.

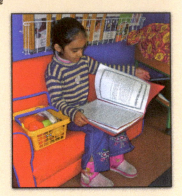

Learning Story 1.1   Kamalpreet Enjoys her Portfolio

Appropriating Knowledges and Learning Dispositions in a Range of Increasingly Complex Ways

This is the fourth theme. A curriculum document may set out a mandated pathway for the appropriation of subject-based knowledge, but for teachers *and* children, the acquisition of that knowledge includes more than 'mastery'. It includes making personal sense of it, making it one's own. We have found James Wertsch's (1997) definition of 'appropriation' useful in this context:

> Since I trace my understanding of appropriation to Bakhtin's writings, it is worth examining the term he employed in Russian: *prisvoenie*. The root of *prisvoenie* and the related verb *prisvoit'* is related to the possessive adjective svoi, which means 'one's own'. *Prisvoit'* means something like to bring something into oneself or to make something one's own, and the noun *prisvoenie* means something like the process of making something one's own ... For my present purposes the point is that making words, including narratives, one's own may be quite distinct from mastering them. (p. 16)

For an extended discussion of 'mutual appropriation', see Brown, Ash, Rutherford, Nakagawa, Gordon and Campione (1993). The 'process of making something one's own' is a process of personalisation. At an early childhood centre that personalisation occurs in a number of ways that include: (i) aligning and adapting the knowledge from home and building on a prior interest; (ii) telling one's story to others and dialoguing about it; and (iii) representing ideas in a range of modes and languages.

Aligning and Adapting the Knowledge from Home and Building on a Prior Interest

Kyah brought resources from home to personalise this concept. We might say that she sees herself as someone whose work can mirror the work of adult fabric designers; in dispositional terms, this story documents what might be an emerging disposition to improvise with materials at hand and to experiment with processes and ideas. Teachers value this and notice, recognise and respond to[3] other examples of it. Kyah brings a constellation of learning dispositions and interests to this task.

Telling One's Story to Others and Dialoguing About it

Marianne was a teacher researcher in the same project as Naomi; here she comments on developing a 'shared history of knowledge' with one of the children:

> I think what happened through the conversations was that, through the funds of knowledge shared in conversations, the funds of disposition were revealed, and became more robust as we had our conversations ... he was actually quite a quiet boy to start with and it was really only through the revisiting that a lot of his stories were revealed. So this kind of left an impression of the power of revisiting for me. ... Through this ritual of revisiting and conversations [over a year], as well as the learning stories perhaps forming the foundations of revisiting, a shared history of knowledge was found.

Representing Ideas in a Range of Modes and Languages

Kyah's story is an example of three of these: the text (read to her) and images from a wearable arts exhibition book provided the inspiration, and a collage. She had already experimented with collage as a medium, cutting out fashion pictures from magazines, and she adapted the idea with a different material, fabric and clothing. In the analysis of the learning, Jenelle commented on the disposition: 'You seem to be of a character that thinks "outside the square", looking for different ways to express an idea and find answers to the questions you have set yourself.' Another Learning Story written by Joanna for Kyah, *The Artists Among Us!*, illustrates her work with another 'language': mosaics (see Learning Story 1.2).

The Artists Among Us!

Teacher: Joanna

To be inspired by an artist! What an incredible privilege and exciting opportunity. For some time we pondered the idea of bringing an expert artist into the centre to work with and alongside the children. [...]

Inspired by our art expert Julie's work and the group mosaic, Kyah embraced the idea of creating her own piece of art. Kyah researched an idea, gazing intently through a library book on mosaic design, before deciding on an idea that she intended to create. After gathering the tools she needed to create her design she was off. She began by making a template. Firstly, she drew her design and then she set to work cutting it out as close to the lines as she possibly could. Some time later, Kyah traced her design onto a plaster-board. She analysed her design, adding finishing touches before beginning her mosaic work with coloured tiles. This is very much a work in progress for Kyah, who began this journey several weeks ago. She revisits her work when the desire arises. Watch this space for updates and further photographs!

We don't believe in restricting children's creativity, rather we allow children to set their own tasks and goals. At times when this may be a challenge, we responsively support and encourage children's endeavours. This process of mosaic-making gave Kyah the opportunity to examine the work of artists in mosaic books, plan her own design, make a template of the ideas that were of most interest to her and take responsibility for all aspects of this process [such as] active research and creative artwork, like tracing her original design onto the surface, selecting the coloured tiles to form her picture and grouting.

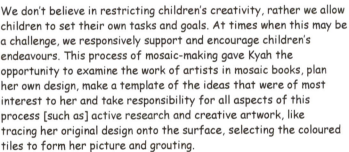

Working alongside Kyah during this process has been such a privilege. Kyah is a passionate, motivated learner who is eager to challenge herself. She is decisive, inspired and works methodically with very clear thoughts and ideas. Kyah's sense of herself as a 'competent and capable learner' has given her the confidence to explore new concepts, challenge her thoughts and ideas and those of others. I believe that learning dispositions (such as getting involved, expressing a thought or idea, taking responsibility, persisting with difficulty and taking an interest) are embedded in the way that Kyah interacts within her environment and in the open and reciprocal relationships she shares.

Learning Story 1.2   The Artists Among Us!

Knowledges and Learning Dispositions

We have described learning as a complex intermingling of *stores* of knowledge[4] with *stores* of disposition. Something similar to this intermingling has been described as *adaptive expertise*: 'that is, the development of flexible knowledge and dispositions that facilitate effective navigation across varied settings and tasks' (Nasir, Rosebery, Warren and Lee, 2006: 490). We look to storying to reflect this complexity.

Dispositions act as an affective and cultural filter for the development of increasingly complex knowledges and skills. They can adhere to a place beyond the home, as a *dispositional milieu*, encouraging or constraining the exploration and construction of new knowledge or ideas. Participating in a new place – an early childhood centre or a school – will usually include taking up that community's perspectives on: the relevance of the knowledge to the world of the child; the opportunity to risk being wrong; the positioning of the learner as one who initiates or one who follows; the enthusiasm with which new ideas and questions are received and explored; and the opportunity to discuss what might be.

Learning dispositions were included as outcomes in the 1996 New Zealand early childhood curriculum. By late 2007, a new New Zealand school curriculum included 'key competencies', influenced by the Organisation for Economic Co-operation and Development (OECD) work in this area (Rychen and Salganik, 2001, 2003). The key competencies are: thinking, using language, symbols and texts; managing self; relating to others; and participating and contributing. Their definition indicates that these are dispositional outcomes:

> More complex than skills, the competencies draw also on knowledge, attitudes, and values in ways that lead to action. They are not separate or stand-alone. They are the key to learning in every learning area …

> The competencies continue to develop over time, shaped by interactions with people, places, ideas and things. Students need to be challenged and supported to develop them in contexts that are increasingly wide-ranging and complex. (Ministry of Education, 2007: 12)

School teachers began to reflect on what these might look like and how they might teach and assess them. Rose Hipkins (2009) writes about the way in which key competencies have introduced new dimensions to learning outcomes and environments: 'meta' knowing; fostering a disposition to learn; empowering students to become experts on their own learning; and rich learning contexts. She adds:

> Over time, students develop personal stories about themselves as learners. Assessment needs to help them build coherent narratives about their identities as people who can practise, persist, and overcome obstacles to immediate learning success. (p. 5)

She suggests that as schools explore ways to teach dispositional outcomes they will need to rethink familiar assessment strategies, and consider newer assessment strategies such as the following: learning logs or journals, learning stories, portfolios and rich tasks. Yvonne S., a teacher writing some reflective comments during a research project exploring how to teach these dispositional outcomes, commented that she wanted to:

> explore how the draft Key Competencies could be integrated into the daily programme, and assessed, without creating extra workload for teachers already struggling with an overloaded curriculum.

In her classroom, portfolios or folders included the children's reading and writing and mathematics progress, and also included Learning Stories that illustrate their progress with the key competencies. The portfolios (sometimes called 'folders' or 'files') for these children included Group Stories, Personalised Group Stories and Individual Stories. Yvonne's Individual Stories, true to the dispositional nature of the Key Competencies, often recorded an event when the learner *chose* their activity. For instance, an Individual Story was written about Abby who initiated a role-playing game in which she was a librarian, issuing books to a small group of willing participants. Yvonne writes: 'This is the first time Abby has instigated an activity and taken a lead role.' A self-comment by Abby soon after this reads, 'I was shy when I started school ... [now] I put my hand up ....' In a Personalised Group Story in which the class were invited to see what they could find out about clouds (entitled *Budding Researchers*), there is a photo of Abby presenting back to the class, with the photo caption 'I did a Google search'.

Another individual story is included as Learning Story 1.3. In Yvonne's and a number of other school classrooms, the Learning Stories are analysed in a 'split-screen' manner (Claxton, Chambers, Powell and Lucas, 2011: 92–96), noting both the knowledge (in this case the school curriculum 'Learning Area': mathematics) and the disposition (in this case the school curriculum key competency: participating and contributing). There are a number of aspects to this short story. Yvonne notes the specific outcome in the curriculum that this story refers to, and she reports that Abagail gave a *detailed explanation* of how she arrived at the answer: explaining and demonstrating with her fingers. She points out why this is a significant episode: Abagail had not been able to explain before. The analysis of the dispositional key competency includes pointing out that she was 'taking risks' to explain. She suggests at the end that Abagail 'sees herself as a mathematician'.

The Chapters of the Book

This chapter has introduced four themes of learner identity and aligned to these themes were four processes in which learner identities in early education are constructed. These themes will weave their way through this book. They provide some of the theoretical assumptions that lead us to the topic of Chapter 2: Why story? That chapter will set out an argument for stories as assessments: consequences of assessment for learning; assessment practice as narrative research, and the development of Learning Stories. Each of the

---

Learning Story - Explaining how to get the answer.

Child: Abagail
Activity/topic: Maths

Date: 20 September
Teacher: Yvonne

Specific Learning Outcomes
Learning how to image when solving addition and subtraction problems to 10.

In maths we have been doing a lot of adds/subtract to 10 by using materials (usually fingers). The children have been introduced to imaging and encouraged to explain how they worked it out. Usually, they would just say, "In my head" or "I counted". Today, Abagail gave a detailed explanation of how she arrived at her answer. She explained and demonstrated with her fingers.

Analysis key competencies
Abagail was showing that she was participating and contributing by being deeply involved in an educational activity, as well as taking risks to explain her way and using mathematical language. She sees herself as being a mathematician.

Analysis Essential Learning Area
Abagail is beginning to image and then explain using materials. This was a breakthrough, as she had not been able to **explain** before.

Where to next
Keep extending this learner to ensure this skill is developed further and move on to counting.

Learning Story 1.3   Explaining How to Get the Answer

following four chapters focuses on one of the four themes, examines the ways in which narrative assessment can contribute to this, and illustrates the ways in which, over the last ten years, Learning Stories have responded to the demands and challenges of: dialogue (Chapter 3), connection (Chapter 4), recognising (Chapter 5) and appropriating (Chapter 6). Chapter 7 considers each of these themes as a balancing and privileging task that will continue to characterise the ongoing quest by the teaching profession to develop assessment practices that work in the interest of education for all.

Notes

1   This frame of 'ready, willing and able' is a key feature of the 2001 book on Learning Stories, introduced there on p. 9 and used as a framework for analysing the learning (generally on p. 24 and for a specific project on p. 124). This book suggests that any one of the ready–willing–able triad can be foregrounded in a particular story. It is a version of the framework for critical thinking by Lauren Resnick (1987: 40–42) and for 'thinking dispositions' by David Perkins, Eileen Jay and Shari Tishman (1993) at Harvard's Project Zero. Also from Project Zero, Ron Ritchhart (2002) has further

expanded on these ideas in a book entitled *Intellectual character: What it is, why it matters, and how to get it*. Ritchhart's book translated 'being able' into knowledge and skills. In this book we have written about the close intermingling of disposition (being ready and willing: the inclination and the attunement to opportunity) and knowledge, thinking of the knowledge as knowing-how as well as knowing-what, both *subject-based* as well as *disposition-based* (for instance, knowing ways to invite others to join in is central to the disposition to work with others). This follows from a project where, with other researchers, we followed case study children from early childhood into school: *Learning in the making: Disposition and design in early education* (Carr, Smith, Duncan, Jones, Lee and Marshall 2010). This book includes a chapter entitled 'Dispositions and positions'. This combination has enabled us to write about split-screen analysis, useful for teachers in school who must clearly assess subject-based knowledge. The notion of 'split-screen' pedagogy has been introduced to teachers at professional development workshops by Guy Claxton, and we have extended it here to refer to assessment. See Claxton, Chambers, Powell and Lucas (2011) for a discussion in detail.

2 New Zealand, Ministry of Education (1996). Other sources of information about this curriculum include a 2003 edited book by Joce Nuttall, *Weaving Te Whāriki*, and a chapter on Te Whāriki by Anne B. Smith (2011) in a book entitled *Theories and approaches to learning in the early years*, edited by Linda Miller and Linda Pound.

3 Noticing, recognising and responding has been used as a definition of assessment in the first of the 20 books in the series *Kei Tua o te Pae Assessment for Learning: Early Childhood Exemplars*. Together with Carolyn Jones, we compiled these books and wrote the text: Carr, Lee and Jones (2004, 2007, 2009). In Book One (2004: 6) we say:

> In this project, assessment for learning is described as 'noticing, recognising and responding'. This description comes from Bronwen Cowie's work on assessment in science classrooms (2000). It was useful to teachers in her study, and we have found it useful as well.

We have described these three processes as progressive filters: teachers notice a great deal as they work with children, and they recognise some of what they notice as 'learning'. They will respond to a selection of what they recognise. Since then we have added two more filters: recording and re-visiting. We will refer to this series of booklets on several occasions in this book. Books 1 to 9 were published in 2004; Books 10 to 15 in 2007, and Books 16 to 20 in 2009. These are available on the New Zealand Ministry of Education website at: http://www.lead.ece.govt.nz/EducateHome/learning/curriculumAndLearning/Assessmentforlearning/KeiTuaotePae.aspx. More details on the development of Kei Tua o te Pae and Te Whāriki are in the first issue of the journal *Assessment matters* (Carr, 2009), and an interesting book on noticing is John Mason's *Researching your own practice: The discipline of noticing* (2002).

4 In this book we have used the expression 'stores' of knowledge and 'stores' of dispositions in preference to 'funds'. In the 2001 book on Learning Stories, the 'being able' part of the dispositional triad 'being ready, willing and able' was described as 'skills and funds of knowledge' (see especially pp. 123–4), and in a project where we researched the children's views about their own learning with teachers in nine early childhood centres, the expression 'funds of disposition' was suggested to parallel 'funds of knowledge'. However, 'funds of knowledge' has a special meaning in the literature: 'We use the term "funds of knowledge" to refer to these historically accumulated and culturally developed bodies of knowledge and skills essential for household or individual functioning and well-being' (Moll, Amanti, Neff, Gonzalez, 1992: 133; also in González, Moll and Amanti, 2005: 169); this expression has come to refer to the knowledge and skills that children bring from home to school (and by extrapolation, to pre-school as well).

2

Why Story?

Box 2.1

As I began to write Learning Stories using the new indicators, I became aware that the stories that really excited me were generally stories that illustrated one or more of the indicators. The significance of this is the fact that I am discovering more about myself as an educator, about the connection between what I value, what I teach, and what I recognise as meaningful learning. The implications of this are twofold. Firstly, this process can empower us as educators. It allows us to explore our own values, attitudes and beliefs and to examine our practice, critiquing its elements and understanding whether or not what we are doing complements our values. This in turn, allows us to shape our practice. (Nikki, teacher in a Year One and Year Two classroom)

Nikki was a teacher researcher on the same practitioner research project as Yvonne S., whose story about Abagail was included in the previous chapter. Nikki and Yvonne were using Learning Stories in their classrooms. This chapter includes data from this project and others to outline the possibilities of Learning Stories as assessment practice. There are three major aspects to this discussion: assessment for learning; assessment practice as narrative research; and the development of Learning Stories.

Assessment for Learning

The most comprehensive review of the research on 'assessment for learning' was published for teachers in a summary publication (1998a) *Inside the black box: Raising standards through classroom assessment* by Paul Black and Dylan

Wiliam at King's College London, University of London. Referring to assessment for learning, Black and Wiliam (1998a) say (emphasis in the original) that in this paper:

> the term 'assessment' refers to all those activities undertaken by teachers, *and by their students in assessing themselves*, which provide information to be used as feedback to modify the teaching and learning activities in which they are engaged. *Such assessment becomes 'formative assessment' when the evidence is actually used to adapt the teaching work to meet the needs.* (p. 2)

Robust research or reviews of research from 250 sources on formative assessment were analysed in detail. The authors point out that all of the studies that they analysed show that 'innovations which include strengthening the practice of formative assessment practice produce significant, and often substantial, learning gains' (ibid.: 3) and that many of the studies showed that 'improved formative assessment helps the (so-called) low attainers more than the rest' (ibid.: 4). The review highlights the value of 'sustained programmes of professional development and support' for this programme, commenting that 'lasting and fundamental improvements in teaching and learning can only happen this way' (ibid.: 15; see also Black and Wiliam, 1998b).

In later work Wiliam and colleagues (2004) worked with secondary teachers to research how to implement these ideas. The key features of formative assessment in action were: questioning (by teachers and pupils), feedback, sharing criteria with learners, self-assessment, and a general category that added 'including parents, posters and presentations' (Wiliam, Lee, Harrison and Black, 2004: 54). In another summary booklet, this time entitled *Working Inside the Black Box* (Black, Harrison, Lee, Marshall and Wiliam, 2002), the authors asked how change can happen. The teachers came to listen to their pupils more attentively and began to appreciate more fully that learning was a process 'in which the learners were active in creating their own understandings' (2002: 15). The authors add that pupils 'came to understand what counted as good work through exemplification' and 'making explicit what was normally implicit' (2002: 15). They cite Carol Dweck's research on roadblocks to learning and link this to classroom cultures: when the classroom culture encourages ego involvement, students focus on the evaluation of their ability and the assessment of their performance; when the culture encourages task involvement, students focus on the task to be done and the effort to improve. Black and colleagues (2002) conclude that: 'In general, feedback given as rewards or grades increases ego – rather than task – involvement. ... Feedback that focuses on what needs to be done can encourage all to believe that they can improve' (p. 19).

Two other writers on formative assessment also cite Dweck and colleagues' research when they write about formative assessment with younger children (primary school children in England aged 5 to 7 years): Harry Torrance and John Pryor (1998) have pointed out that young children are just developing their ideas about ability and effort, and the criteria for good work, and that the giving or withholding of extrinsic rewards as the formative aspect of an assessment does not assist this development:

> The children in this study are still young (the oldest are 7). Their experience of what constitutes good work is limited, and their capacity to differentiate between difficulty, ability and effort is, at the least, underdeveloped. The availability of an easy way of telling whether or not work is good enough through the giving or withholding of extrinsic reward means that they are not encouraged to think about criteria in any principled way. (p. 105)

Carol Dweck (2006), early in her book entitled *Mindset*, described children who enjoyed a difficult task: 'What did they know? They knew that human qualities such as intellectual skills, could be cultivated with effort' (p. 4). They took responsibility to confront a challenge and recognised that struggles, mistakes and perseverance were part of the picture. The teachers in our research and professional projects were also referencing the theoretical literature, often in the text of their Learning Stories, in order to make connections to research and their favourite writers from the past to point the way towards possible learner selves. In Chapter 1, Karen H. referred to Guy Claxton's (2004) work on 'Learning is learnable' to describe the context for Kyah's learning. In a Learning Story about Keira, Melissa has highlighted the research by Carol Dweck on growth mindset (see Learning Story 2.1). In her analysis of the learning, Melissa comments on the willingness of the children at her centre to grow their intelligence by stretching and challenging their minds, and she references Dweck's ideas.[1]

Two years earlier, another Learning Story about Keira by Karen H., enjoying an unexpected downpour of rain, included a quote from Mihaly Csikszentmihalyi (1996: 361): 'Good scientists, like good artists, must let their minds roam playfully or they will not discover new facts, new relationships. At the same time they must be able to evaluate critically every novelty they encounter ...'. These references to writers and researchers, together with the teachers' commentary on the children's learning over time, describe the philosophy of this centre, linking that philosophy clearly to an example of practice. The portfolio reflects a continuity of purpose and value in this learning environment; it sends messages to the family and to Keira about the learner qualities that are valued, and the practices that afford and support those qualities.

Nikki and her co-teacher, Susie, had been encouraging the students in their school classroom to gain an appreciation of 'good' work with reference to

Growth Mindset

"In a growth mindset, people believe that their most basic abilities can be developed through dedication and hard work—brains and talent are just the starting point. This view creates a love of learning and a resilience that is essential for great accomplishment. Virtually all great people have had these qualities."

Carol Dweck - *mindsetonline.com*

In Te Whare Aotūroa we have a wooden figure that stands on a plinth. This figure is available for the children to use when visualising the human form in their art. I had moved it to the table for a moment while I was shifting something else and Keira was very interested in its purpose. A group of children stopped to listen in on our discussion so I showed them how the arms and legs could be moved to the shape the artist wanted to draw. We discussed the different parts of the body and when I asked the children if they were interested in having a go, everyone moved off, except for Keira, who quickly found a piece of paper and a pencil.

Working independently, Keira soon had a head, neck, upper torso, lower torso, arms and legs on her figure. She stopped after she made each addition to the sketch, studied the figurine and decided on the next shape needed.

Soon, Keira had her first figure finished and she moved on to a second. Once again she worked with great concentration.

(Continued)

(Continued)

What learning happened here for Keira?

The teachers at Greerton have been very interested in the theories of Carol Dweck for some time now. Day by day we see examples of her research in the work we do with the children here at Mitchell St. Carol Dweck calls this a "Growth Mindset"; where one views their intelligence as an ever–expanding repertoire of skills and knowledge.

Today I saw this disposition to be challenged in Keira. Her curiosity to notice and be interested in the figure opened up the possibility for her to be a learner in a new situation. I think this is fabulous! Her willingness is even more interesting when we note that the other children in the room backed away from the challenge – for various reasons perhaps – but Keira was not influenced by them. She showed that she is the master of her own learning. Keira showed courage, independence and great mathematical skills as she drew her figures. I'm interested to see where this work leads her next. I wonder if she will continue to refine her drawings of figurines?

Teacher: Melissa   Date: August

Learning Story 2.1   Growth Mindset

key competencies (see Chapter 1, p.15). They consulted the children as they were developing indicators for the key competencies, soon to become mandatory in the 2007 school curriculum. The five- and six-year-olds in their combined Year One and Year Two classrooms brainstormed about the key competency 'relating to others' and developed the following list: treating others as you would like to be treated; letting people join in, thanking people that help you, sitting next to someone new, listening to people, showing new people around the school. The children were appropriating these outcomes – in the sense defined by Wertsch and outlined in the previous chapter – by making them their own. Nikki went on to consult the other teachers at the school as well. In the Final Report for this research project, Nikki comments:

> If the team of teachers at each school were to develop their own indicators that reflected the values of the school (in consultation with their community), the values of the teachers and the values of the tamariki [children], imagine how powerful an exercise this could be. (Carr, Peters, Davis, Bartlett, Bashford et al., 2008: 18)

A Learning Story in Box 2.2 is written by Susie, about the brainstorm for another key competency: participating and contributing. It is followed by a teaching task that built from this event.

Box 2.2

What does 'participation' look like?

A Learning Story written for the class by Susie

Today we dialogued with the children on the school-wide focus of 'participation'. First we talked about the word, looked it up in the dictionary and then asked the children for their thoughts, comments, examples or questions (see brainstorm posters). Some of the children talked about trying something new, giving something a go, getting involved, helping others etc. ... We finished the workshop with a discussion on how the children had felt about participating in the game and talked further about trying new things this term. Many of the children were already starting to use the word *participation* in context.

Analysis: the children used the competency language as they interpreted and understood the dialogue we had around participation. This was shown in their questions, comments and examples of what they had learnt or discovered about participation. Key Competency cues were highlighted.

Possible Next Steps: Next week to continue to look at the word *participation* and try something they don't usually do.

[The next week the class did indeed try activities that they didn't usually participate in, and the children brainstormed how it made them feel (see the whiteboard record). Susie wrote another class story about this event.]

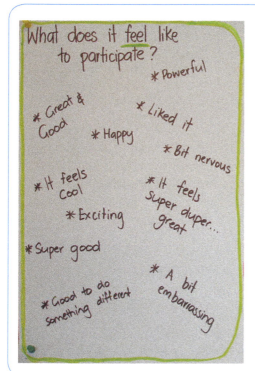

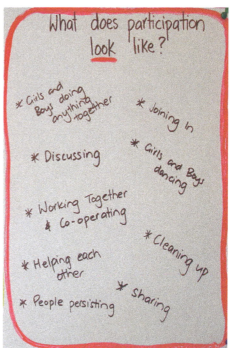

A differentiation between 'convergent' and 'divergent' formative assessment is made by Torrance and Pryor (1998: 152–9). Convergent assessment is accomplished mainly by the teacher. It starts from the aim to discover *if* the learner knows, understands or can do a predetermined thing. Characteristics include: precise planning by the teacher and an intention to stick to it; recording via checklists and can-do statements; closed or pseudo-open teacher questioning and tasks.

Divergent assessment is accomplished mainly via a collaboration between and amongst teachers and students. It starts from the aim to discover *what* the learner knows, understands or can do. Characteristics include: flexible planning or complex planning that incorporates alternatives; open forms of recording (narrative, quotations, etc.); primarily open tasks with questioning by teachers and learners directed at 'helping' rather than at testing. A connection might be made here to the two major dimensions of *adaptive expertise*, introduced in Chapter 1: processes that lead to *innovation* or invention are encouraged by divergent assessment processes; processes that lead to *efficiency* through well-practised routines are encouraged by convergent assessment processes. A paper by John Pryor and Barbara Crossouard (2008) emphasises identity. They say that:

> Formative assessment is seen as taking place when teachers and learners seek to respond to student work, making judgements about what is good learning. However, acknowledging learning as being bound up with identity construction (Lave & Wenger, 1991; Holland et al., 1998) implies that formative assessment interactions involve enabling learners first to engage with new ways of being and acting associated with new, aspirational identities; and second to have these recognised as legitimate, where what counts as legitimate is strongly framed by institutional discourses and assessment demands. (p. 3)

In a story entitled *Little Miss Scientist* (see Learning Story 2.2), the narrative emphasises the way in which Leilani has engaged in what may be a new way of being and acting, as a scientist. This possible self, or aspirational identity, is legitimated by the teacher and the family, who confirm the assessment about Leilani's interest and her curiosity, and add that she could report 'in great detail' about a science trip.

A 2009 document prepared for the New Zealand Ministry of Education entitled 'Directions for Assessment in New Zealand' (Absolum, Flockton, Hattie, Hipkins and Reid, 2009) includes a section on 'Valid interpretations and decisions'. The authors say:

> When we use the term valid, we mean that the descriptive (scores, levels, observations, etc.) and prescriptive (what to do next) interpretations and inferences made are defensible in their consequences. It is not the test, test score, or observation that is validated so much as the decisions and actions that flow from the test, score, or observation. Validity is a function of both parts of the decision-making process: if the descriptive part is good but the prescriptive part is poor (in other words, if the student's performance is correctly determined but consequential decisions are detrimental to learning) or vice versa, the assessment lacks validity … Our concern is the extent to which the accumulated evidence supports a particular interpretation or decision. Ultimately, a lot depends on informed professional judgement, so the more effort we put into strengthening the teachers' assessment capabilities, and the greater the effort that teachers put into strengthening students' assessment capabilities, the more we can expect that interpretations and consequential actions will be valid. (p. 33)

In this book, the consequences that we are interested in highlighting are the four learner-identity themes that we set out in the previous chapter: agency and dialogue; making connections across boundaries between places; recognising and re-cognising learning continuities; and appropriating knowledges and learning dispositions in a range of increasingly complex ways. We placed these four consequences 'in the middle' between the learner and the learning environment in any educational setting. The affordance network[2] for these processes includes the teacher, the prior learning and expectations of the students, the artifacts (resources and assessment practices realised in portfolios, tests, certificates, charts and graphs), the ways in which teachers and learners are positioned in relation to each other, the routines and tasks, and the wider community beyond the early childhood setting or classroom (the

What a great day we all had at Science Alive. Firstly, we had a chance to do some experiments in the classroom and then we went through to the interactive area. Leilani, I noticed that you were keen to take part in all the experiments and that you were able to answer some tricky questions about floating and sinking, solids and liquids, gases and dissolving. You followed the instructions carefully when you were asked to do something by the parent helpers and thought about what you had observed, before sharing it with others.

What does this tell me?
This tells me that you are actively involved in your learning and that you are motivated to participate in all activities. You worked really well with the other children. I was impressed with the great thinking skills you used and how you used your "Stop and Think" Habit of Mind to answer questions confidently. Well done Leilani!

Where to next?
I can tell that you are curious about the world around you and that you are keen to learn more. You might be able to find some interesting books in the library to look at. We will be doing some more science topics and experiments during the year, so I look forward to hearing you share your great ideas again.

Leilani's voice:
"I had fun at Science Live."

Parent's voice:
Did Leilani tell you about our visit to Science Alive?

"Yes Leilani did tell us about the Science Alive trip in great detail and she told everybody who came to visit our home about the trip too. Leilani loves Science Alive and always asks to visit if we are driving past or wanting to have a day trip out. Leilani is very curious about the world and how things work."

---

school, the families, the society and the economy).[3] An assessment practice may afford or deny opportunities for initiative and dialogue, be more or less permeable (providing space for, or silencing, the inclusion of other perspectives and other communities), enhance or disrupt the recognition of legitimate longer-term learning pathways, and either acknowledge and celebrate the complexity of learning or focus only on the certain and the narrow.

Assessment Practice as Narrative Research

Researchers with Paul Black have had something to say about the assessment of these learning strategies and dispositions as well: in an Assessment for Learning How to Learn (LHTL) project (Black, McCormick, James and Pedder, 2006), the researchers trialled a two-task sequence that focused on assessing pupils' development of 'learning how to learn'. They concluded (p. 130) that qualitative methods may be more appropriate: 'A better alternative might be to develop critical indicators to identify LHTL achievement during normal classroom work, and for teachers to use these in a running record of their pupils' work, over time and across a variety of contexts.' We translate this notion of a 'running record' across a variety of contexts as a sequence of *stories* about learning. An early record of Alex's Learning How to Learn strategies is in the story *Researcher!* (see Learning Story 2.3).

Alex   July   # Researcher!

Alex has a great passion for puddles and can source them out like a bloodhound!
It is not only puddles that Alex has a strong interest in researching, but also MUDDY puddles.
His research requires him to get as close as possible to his interest. He uses all the resources at hand to investigate fully. His most important research tools are his hands, which he loves to splash in the puddles. The fact that Alex is getting wet or, as in the photo, muddy, doesn't bother him. Alex's senses give him a lot of information about puddles and it is through these that he is identifying properties of water; it's wet, slippery, hard to hold and, when mixed with dirt, it changes to make mud. I get the impression that Alex feels these creations of nature need a lot more studying!

Learning Story 2.3   Researcher!

The 2001 book *Learning Stories* (Carr, 2001a) included a quote from Elliot Eisner, an artist and writer on education, to exemplify the view that teachers get to know their students in a variety of contexts and that 'short narratives' would provide a more personalised and replete picture of achievement:

> Teachers are in a position to interpret the quality of the student's questions, the insight of his or her answers, the degree of engagement they display in doing their work, the quality of their relationship with other students, the level of imagination they attain; these and a host of other personal factors are qualities that teachers can know about. These features, as they emerge in classroom life, ought to be a primary source of data for understanding what students are learning and how far they have come along since the beginning of the school year.
>
> As researchers, we need to design practices in which teachers pay systematic attention to such features and prepare short narratives that would provide a much more replete picture of achievement than a B+ or an 82 on a standardised achievement test. (Eisner, 2000: 350–1)

Eisner emphasises the following learning outcomes: insightful answers, a high level of engagement, quality relationships and imagination. These outcomes are a complex intermingling of knowledges and dispositions.

Teachers as Researchers, Research as Narrative

An increasing recognition of the value of teacher researchers – and teachers as researchers in their everyday professional lives – has been reflected in the rapid growth of action research or practitioner inquiry projects, in which teacher researchers and university researchers work together to investigate and theorise educational practice. Marilyn Cochran-Smith and Kelly Donnell (2006) use the term 'practitioner inquiry' to refer to 'the array of educational research genres where the practitioner is the researcher, the professional context is the research site, and practice itself is the focus of study' (p. 503). In our experience, teachers in practitioner inquiry projects develop theory as well; Cochran-Smith and Donnell add that 'practitioners are amongst those who have the authority to construct Knowledge (with a capital K) about teaching and learning' (p. 508), and we agree. Writing about 'Reform through action research', Davydd Greenwood and Morten Levin (2008) comment that:

> Action research aims to solve pertinent problems in a given context through demo-cratic inquiry in which professional researchers collaborate with local stakeholders [*in our case, teachers*] to seek and enact solutions to problems of major importance to the stake-holders. We refer to this as cogenerative inquiry … The professional researcher often brings knowledge of other relevant cases and of relevant research methods, and he or she often has experience in organizing research processes. The insiders have extensive and long-term knowledge of the problems at hand and the contexts in which they occur, as well as knowledge about how and from whom to get additional information. (p. 72)

In the action research projects where we have been participants, teachers have often added reflective comments to their observations, frequently referring to theorists that the 'outsider' researchers have offered because they seem to have something to say about the 'problem at hand'. In a reflection as part of an action research project, Lorraine adds some comments on the role of Learning Stories in enabling teachers to 'figure out' the underlying 'institutional discourses' about learning that Pryor and Crossouard talked about:

> I think from the increasing body of narrative examples and reflections in our centre, that we are becoming a great deal better at 'figuring out' just what it means to be immersed in a culture that values investigative research as a way of uncovering meaning and building working theories. For a long time now we have shifted the power base to a place where children are in charge of their learning within the parameters of a socially connected group. (Lorraine, teacher)

In a related commentary on learning outcomes in curriculum, also reminiscent of the work of Nikki and Susie in their Year One and Year Two classroom, Andy Hargreaves and Shawn Moore (2000) have argued strongly that a huge level of discretion should be granted to teachers and local initiatives when outcomes are complex: 'these possibilities include fostering stronger collegiality among teachers, and democratic inclusion of pupils and parents in the teaching and learning process' (p. 27). Writing in the 1990s about research with teachers teaching an Ontario curriculum that listed 10 broad Essential Learning Outcomes the comment was made that 'One way for teachers to make outcomes real in, and learning relevant to, the lives of their students, was to share the learning outcomes openly and explicitly with their students' (p. 37). We saw that Nikki and Susie consulted their Year One and Year Two students about their understanding of the new (at the time, draft) key competencies, and they then included some of their ideas as indicators of the key competencies in their Learning Story protocols.

Chapter 1 in Jean Clandinin's 2007 edited *Handbook of narrative inquiry* sets out what is described as the historical 'turns to narrative' in relation to assumptions about knowledge and knowing. One of these is 'objectivity': 'What fundamentally distinguishes the narrative turn from "scientific" objectivity is understanding that knowing other people and their interactions is always a relational process that ultimately involves caring for, curiosity, interest, passion, and change' (Pinnegar and Daynes, 2007: 29). Classrooms and early childhood centres are complex places. They have been described as complex and diverse environments that 'present a wilderness of vaguely marked and ill-defined occasions for thoughtful engagement' (Perkins, Tishman, Ritchhart, Donis and Andrade, 2000: 270). The example *Super Story Writer* illustrates a range of interpretive voices: Molly dictates that she likes doing her best writing and that she likes writing about flowers, and a parent adds another dimension of this emergent self in a comment on Molly's writing of notes at home (see Learning Story 2.4).

Super Story Writer

Each morning the Room 2 children practise their story writing. We have been learning how to write sentences correctly. Molly, I noticed how well you were working on Wednesday morning. You got busy and drew a picture plan before writing your story.

I was impressed with the three different sentences you were able to write on your own. You remembered capital letters, full stops and spacing. You also read your sentences to make sure that they made sense. It is great to see that you are learning how to spell lots of words and that you are also beginning to use a word card to find other words. Well done! What an enthusiastic writer you are!

What does this tell me?
This tells me that you are developing independence in your story writing. You are able to express your ideas clearly in sentences and link your ideas together to give the reader more information (**Being clear;** Habit of Mind). You are also very **Persistent** and always make sure that your work is completed.

Where to next?
Very soon you will be using a book that does not need a picture plan. Then you will be able to get started straight away with your story ideas. I am looking forward to seeing lots of other interesting stories this year. Keep up the good effort with your spelling words too.

Molly's voice:
I like doing my best writing, and writing about pretty flowers.

Parent's voice:
Molly often writes lovely little notes at home. She is very good at trying, without asking for help. You are so wonderful at your writing Molly!

Learning Story 2.4   Super Story Writer

Research and Story

Vivian Gussin Paley's writing over many years of teaching young children has been a significant inspiration to both of us, and to the teachers with whom we have worked. Her books have provided powerful arguments and illustrations of the role of story in the construction of self, and of the necessary connection between a theory of learning and a way of teaching. She describes stories that the children dictate and then act out with their peers at the end of a session; they become the topic of conversation with peers and Paley. In her 'A child's work' she makes her view of learning clear:

> If readiness for school has meaning, it is to be found first in the children's flow of ideas, their own and those of their peers, families, teachers, books, and television, from play into story and back into more play. It was when I asked the children to dictate their stories and bring them to life again on a stage that the connections between play and analytical thinking became clear. The children and I were nourishing the ground and opening the seed packets, ready to plant our garden of ideas and identities. (Paley, 2004: 11–12)

She connects the stories with what happens next: children 'bringing them to life again on a stage' so that the connections between play and analytical thinking became clear. In Susie and Nikki's class portfolios, the students workshopped 'trying something new' as an indicator of the key competency 'participation'. Paley's ideas about the analytical thinking associated with skills at story-telling appear to be supported by research on the mathematical gains from Learning Stories (Perry, Dockett and Harly, 2007).

A body of research literature from developmental psychologists Katherine Nelson and others has argued that those young children who have, at home, been engaged in story-telling and story-sharing – conversations about past events – develop personal memories that contribute to identity construction. Nelson (2000) says that the research on young children's construction of personal memories 'indicates that children learn about themselves and construct their self-stories through the medium of narrativising experience with others' (p. 192). Amy Bird and Elaine Reese (2006) have contributed to this body of research about the nature of parent–child conversations about past events by outlining the possible shape of the link between narrative and the self: (i) the stories (and the conversations that develop them) provide a medium for evaluation that communicates the self-relevance of an experience; (ii) talking about stories in the past can take the 'heat' out of emotional aspects; (iii) the use of personal pronouns means that a story represents the self versus others ('my' experience as distinct from 'yours') and (iv) adults can assist children to interpret the stories. Chapter 3 adds data on teacher–learner discussions about Learning Stories to suggest that these research findings may be just as relevant for children and teachers in early childhood provision outside the home.

Elaine Reese and colleagues (2010) also make a link between storying and reading ability. They comment:

> The aspect of oral narrative skill that was most predictive of reading in our study was narrative quality. Note that previous studies with a similar age group sometimes failed to find a unique link between oral narrative and reading, but those studies only tapped story memory, not quality (e.g., Roth, Speece, and Cooper, 2002). Story memory does appear to be a vital indicator of oral narrative skill, especially in the

preschool years … but by primary school, it appears that narrative quality is also important. The specific aspect of narrative quality that correlated with reading performance across both of our studies was orientations, which tap children's ability to introduce characters and to provide temporal, causal, and locative information in their narratives. A child who uses orienting information in a narrative is demonstrating their understanding for critical contextual elements and causal-temporal links in the storyline … It is possible that assessment in the school environment inhibits children's story retelling to some degree. (Reese, Suggate and Long, 2010: p. 641–2)

There is a lesson to be learned for early years practice in schools in their final comment that 'It is possible that assessment in the school environment inhibits children's story retelling to some degree'. At Nikki and Susie's school, storytelling is common; two of Nikki's stories are included in Box 2.3.

Box 2.3

Stories about Diana 'doing something she had never done before'

Making a decision about a workshop

Story: When the children were deciding what workshops they would like to be part of, Diana came up to me and said 'I have picked Te Reo [Māori language] because that is something I have never done before'.

Analysis: The week before this Diana had been part of a Homebase [classroom] discussion on 'participation'. One of the ideas that came up was doing something you had never done before. This story is an example of Diana making a decision with this in mind.

The first Te Reo workshop

Story (for four children): Today we had our first Te Reo workshop. We began by singing a waiata. I had written the words on a chart for the tamariki and we practised singing the different vowel sounds. When we came to the verse, I drew a little picture of a cloud to remind us of the meaning of Aotearoa. After a few times through, Diana said, 'We could make up books with paper and staples and write our song in them. We could put pictures in and write what the words mean. We could all sing it together from our own books'. Phoenix added, 'Then we could practise at home.' I quickly grabbed a piece of paper and started to record their ideas. The ideas kept on flowing … it was decided by the group that we would go to the beach to collect shells and other things to decorate our books. At one point somebody said that we should write a list of things to take to the beach. Diana said we might need to take warm clothes

(Continued)

(Continued)

and that if we watched Prime News at 5.30 we can find out what the weather would be like. …

Analysis: This was such an involved session. The children had great enthusiasm for the subject. They initiated a brainstorm full of ideas and made connections with their prior learning. (*Nikki highlighted the Key Competency cues in the Learning Story format, and noted that this was in the context of the Learning Area 'Learning Languages'.*)

Possible next steps

The beach visit, the making of books and a copy of the waiata for the class.

The Development of Learning Stories

Learning Stories might be described as an 'identity-referenced' assessment practice (Carr, 2005: 46) rather than a norm- or criterion-referenced assessment practice, and the discussion in Chapter 1 supports that view. Nikki describes an identity-referenced assessment when she comments on assessments that highlight a long-term vision of an 'empowered learner':

> I feel comfortable using the Key Competencies with Learning Stories as both enable me to capture learning as it occurs naturally. The Key Competencies lead beyond the learning of discrete skills and towards the bigger picture, honouring the values, attitudes and dispositions that help us become empowered learners in and out of school. (Nikki, teacher)

The story of the development of Learning Stories, following on from the development of the New Zealand national early childhood curriculum is told in the 2001 Learning Story book.[4] When in 1998 our research questioned how to assess new curriculum outcomes that included learning dispositions, teachers asked: Why Not Story? After all, this was how the early years teachers we worked with then informally reported back to families about their children's well-being and progress. Teachers in five very different early childhood programmes trialled an assessment story approach: learning episodes that were annotated to highlight the learning and to add suggestions about the next steps. Early stories were structured around five actions, developed from the five curriculum strands and described as an accumulating story line: taking an interest, being involved, persisting with difficulty, communicating with others, and taking responsibility. These actions were seen as the 'tips of icebergs' of the curriculum strands in the national curriculum. The early stories were usually written by hand, and did not include photographs; at that time teachers were unlikely to have ready access to computers, and digital cameras were still to be developed. A story in one of these formats is included here (see Learning Story 2.5).

Child's name .....George.......
Teacher: ....Jo..............
Date: ......20.7:.........

Learning Story

		Examples or cues	**A LEARNING STORY**
belonging mana whenua	**TAKING AN INTEREST**	Finding an interest *here* – a topic, an activity, a role. Recognising the familiar, enjoying the unfamiliar. Coping with change.	George had the bird for the holidays and was very concerned when he came back that his cage was too small.
well-being mana atua	**BEING INVOLVED**	Paying attention for a sustained period, feeling safe, trusting others. Being playful with others and/or materials.	We decided that making one would be a good idea. George drew a plan and then we talked about what materials we would need to buy to make it.
exploration mana aotūroa	**PERSISTING WITH DIFFICULTY**	Setting and choosing difficult tasks. Using a range of strategies to solve problems when 'stuck' (be specific).	
communication mana reo	**EXPRESSING AN IDEA OR A FEELING**	In a range of ways (specify). For example: oral language, gesture, music, art, writing, using numbers and patterns, telling stories.	We wrote a list of things to make it and used the tape measure to work out how long each piece of wood would be; we decided on 140cm long and 60cm wide.
contribution mana tangata	**TAKING RESPONSIBILITY**	Responding to others, to stories, and imagined events, ensuring that things are fair, self-evaluating, helping others, contributing to programme.	We are going to use wire netting and we need to get hinges for the door.

Short Term Review	**What Next?**
Maths concepts – measuring – numbers Drawing of a plan Taking on a long term project Concern for the well-being of an animal. Question: What learning did I think went on here (i.e. the main point(s) of the learning story)?	I will buy the materials needed for the bird cage and we will begin to make it next week. Questions: How might we encourage this interest, ability, strategy, disposition, story to • Be more complex. • Appear in different areas or activities in the programme. How might we encourage the next 'step' in the learning story framework?

Learning Story 2.5   George

The presentation and *formative* assessment opportunities of Learning Stories have been rapidly transformed by revolutionary changes in information communication technology. In a 1998 video series on assessment, we were all very excited by the affordances of the Polaroid camera: one of the teachers in that video series comments: 'It's just so *instant*!' A mere five or so years later, teachers were responding to the new technological opportunities to write Learning Stories very quickly after the event and to experiment with format and layout (Lee, Hatherly and Ramsey, 2002; Colbert, 2006).

Catherine Reissman (2008: 14) points out that this is a further reason for the narrative 'turn' in research: the affordance of new technologies and the salience of visual texts. These affordances have dramatically enhanced the opportunities for narrative assessments as well. Digital story-telling by young adults has provided eloquent reflections of the views of self that the teller wishes to tell (see Glynda Hull's work, for instance, Hull and Katz, 2006) and for the very young, the ease of digital photography has provided new ways of contributing to their own assessments: taking their own photographs, being able to 'read' assessments, and setting up visual cues for remembering after the event. These new information communication technologies enable Learning Stories to document both vividly and quickly the range of multimodal pathways and affordance networks that have always characterised the early childhood educational environments. Photographs and DVDs capture drawing, painting, three-dimensional constructions, gesture, drama, movement, digital imagery, often in progress. A number of Learning Stories are developed from DVDs, and a number of stories *are* DVDs, as we will see later in Chapter 6.

An early childhood teacher, Julie, reported that a mother returned to the early childhood centre after taking her child's DVD home and said, laughing: 'I've watched that video eleven times. I'm over it now!' Children who are just beginning to construct a narrative with a beginning, a middle and an end, are greatly assisted by photographs in sequence and movies of events to which they can return. The photographs in a story entitled *Home Maker in Action*, where Labeeqa made some tomato relish at the kindergarten is a good example of a sequence of events that can be read by the child (see Learning Story 2.6). A parent wrote this response:

> Hi, today Labeeqa made her tomato relish in her kindergarten. She was very excited and telling everyone about her creation at kindy. She was telling me whole recipe and the method also. We were very happy that she is very keen in cooking and about her recipe. She told me that you need tomatoes, capsicums, vinegar, and onions all the ingredients then you have to cook on stove and then you have to wait to cool down the relish so you can taste it.
>
> Labeeqa brought her relish today from kindergarten and really it was yummmmm-mmm......... We all liked it. She chose the big bottle and made the label also with her

Home Maker in Action

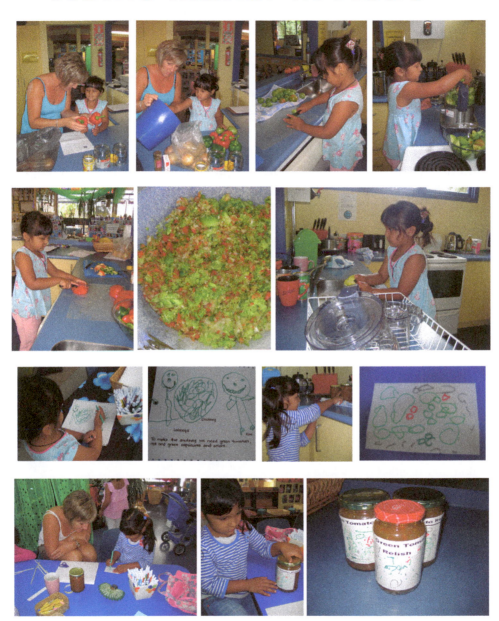

Learning Story 2.6   Home Maker in Action

drawing. We are very happy to this and all other activities with the kids that you guys do that develop the confidence in the children. Keep it up! You guys are great helping our kids grow! Thankyou.

Concluding Comments

Reviewing a number of research studies on the social and cultural complexities of 'learning careers', Katherine Ecclestone and John Pryor (2003) conclude that:

> Taken together, these studies suggest that different assessment systems have an important impact on learning identities and dispositions as children become young adults and then adult 'returners' in an increasingly long life of formal learning. (p. 472)

The series of Learning Stories about Diana, 'doing something she had never-done before' in a number of contexts, reflects an assessment system that is designed to have an impact on learning identities and dispositions. One notable event was Diana's mother also deciding to 'give new things a go'. At school camp Diana's mother thought about the school-wide focus on participation and volunteered to be a model for the children to paint. She was turned into a colourful fox by six eager children. The teachers documented this, concluding, 'Congratulations Natalia, for showing us all a fabulous example of participation!' This chapter includes (Box 2.4) a final Learning Story in the series about Diana.

Box 2.4

Trying something new: A story by Nikki

Today Diana told me she had been thinking about the word participation and decided to try karate for her 'making things, doing things' workshop. She said she was the only girl from her Homebase [classroom] to attend this workshop but thought it was okay because she was trying something new.

She said, 'I was a little scared of the kids from other Homebases [classrooms] but then I wasn't. I kept on doing it and it didn't make me feel nervous anymore. There is one girl in the karate workshop. I remember her from camp. She got her face painted when I was with my mum. That was when we painted my mum.'

> *Analysis:* Diana is developing a strong understanding of the word participation. She is doing this by actively exploring what it means to participate. Diana's risk-taking and her sense of belonging is helping her to trust herself and others, even when she feels scared or nervous.

Nikki was utilising the power of story in other ways in this combined Year One and Year Two classroom. As do all teachers, she reads stories to groups, and she encourages the class to appropriate, to make sense of, the stories for themselves. On one occasion she read a story entitled *Keep Trying* (by Jane Buxton, 2002) about a boy learning to ride a bicycle. One of the children makes a comment during the story, comparing the story about learning to ride a bicycle to her own context of Highland dancing:

> *Nikki*: ... and you can see Dad's here supporting him when he's learning to ride. It's always good to have someone helping you when you're learning new things and guiding you through.
>
> *Student*: That's what I needed in my Highland dancing because Highland dancing is really hard. If you ask me, the teachers keep supporting me in my Highland dancing and soon I'll be able to get up on stage at school maybe and show you the Highland Fling.

This dialogue illustrates some of the themes of the next four chapters, introduced in this chapter as an affordance network (see notes 2 and 3 at the end of this chapter). Nikki and the Highland Fling novice are constructing an authoring learner who responds with enthusiasm to challenge and is supported by others, makes a connection across the boundaries of place, imagines an aspirational identity and a recognition of the journey to get there. Nikki has an appropriating strategy for this complex interweaving of disposition and knowledge: storying.

Notes

1 Carol Dweck's work comes from the field of motivation and personality psychology, and many years of research. As we see in this chapter, her work has been very influential in the field of education and assessment. More detail of her research can be found in her 2006 book *Mindset* and her 2000 book *Self-theories*. For a more socio-cultural perspective on these ideas see Carr (2001b).

2 A definition of 'affordance' is given by James Gee on page 81 of Pamela Moss and others' 2008 edited book on assessment, picking up the notion that knowledge and learning is sited in the relationship between an individual and an environment:

> Any environment in which an individual finds him or herself is filled with affordances. The term 'affordance' (coined by Gibson 1977, 1979; see also Norman 1988) is used to describe the perceived *action possibilities* posed by objects or features in the environment ... Of course, an affordance does not

exist for an individual who cannot perceive its presence. Even when an affordance is recognized, however, a human actor must also have the capacity to transform the affordance into an actual and effective action. (Gee, 2008: 81)

3 These aspects of an affordance network have some parallels with the four aspects of activity theory: instruments, division of labour, community and rules. An example of activity theory in relation to assessment is outlined in Yrjö Engeström, Ritva Engeström and Arja Suntio's chapter in Gordon Wells and Guy Claxton's *Learning for life in the 21st century* (2002). John Pryor and Barbara Crossouard (2008) also apply activity theory in a discussion of 'a socio-cultural theorisation of formative assessment' with learners' and teachers' identities as the intended outcome. In Chapter 4, the main setting will be an Auckland Kindergarten, and in the final report for that research project we used activity theory to describe the affordance network (Ramsey, Breen, Sturm, Lee and Carr, 2006). However, one of the key processes in activity theory is the dynamic tensions at play between the four elements of the network and we have not foregrounded that process in this book. Pryor and Crossouard (2008) do; they point out, for instance, that 'The different identities of the educator as assessor, teacher, subject expert, and learner all involve different divisions of labour and rules shaping their interaction with students' (p. 10). They point out that this is a slightly different 'take' on activity theory since it 'renders unstable what is often seen as a relatively stable part of the activity system: the object or the outcome, which in their activity system is 'learning the renegotiation of identities'.

4 For more on the early development of Learning Stories, and some early examples, see the 2001 Learning Story book (Carr, 2001a) and Chapter 7 by Margaret Carr, Ann Hatherly, Wendy Lee and Karen Ramsey entitled 'Te Whāriki and assessment: A case study of teacher change' (Nuttall, 2003). Refer to note 3 in Chapter 1 for comments on the paper in *Assessment matters* (Carr, 2009), and the *Kei Tua o te Pae* collection. Three videos and a professional development booklet were prepared for teachers in 1998; these have been republished as DVDs (Carr, 1998).

Agency and Dialogue

Box 3.1

When Zeb brought his sharks in to kindy I was amazed at the level of curiosity. There was an element of mystery and intrigue as the children explored these creatures, sharing their thoughts and ideas with one another ... The level of interest was contagious, with curiosity getting the better of all of us in some way. (Teacher reflection from Jackie)

Assessments and patterns of interactions associated with them will position learners in encouraging or discouraging ways, strengthening or diminishing the courage to take over some of the responsibility for their own learning and their own assessment. Writing about assessment practices as one of the opportunities to learn in a classroom, James Greeno and Melissa Gresalfi (2008) comment on the fairly stable patterns of interaction and participation that develop in a classroom over time:

> In an activity setting that extends over time, such as a classroom, patterns of interaction develop such that the ways that different individuals participate have some degree of stability. In our work so far we have found the concept of participatory identity (Holland et al 1998) to be particularly useful in considering students' patterns of participation over time. Identity formation, as we understand it, is a two-way process between the individual and what he or she brings to an interaction and the resources and consequent opportunities of a particular activity setting. (p. 184)

Shared interactions or dialogue, where all the participants share some of the agency may be rare, as the comment by Iram Siraj-Blatchford (2010) in Chapter 1 illustrated. Children may struggle to make sense of the topic and the intent of a conversation with a teacher (Tizard and Hughes, 1984; Carr, 2000). The teachers in what we called the *Learning Wisdom* project found that

Learning Stories can become a jointly owned tool for sustained shared thinking about learning and about whatever comes to mind. In those centres where it is common practice to look back over an earlier Learning Story, it makes sense to talk about a previous event with the main actors in the story. The photographs provide cues for a conversation. After revisiting the portfolios with a number of children, and developing conversations about their learning, Prue, a teacher who also appeared in Chapter 1 (p.11), reflected on the language of learning and some of the pitfalls:

> We are noting a general change in the children's language and often hear conversations which include the following phrases and words: practising, learning, thinking, using my brain. This has transpired in a relatively short space of time and I think it can be attributed to our/the teachers' focus and conscious choice of language. However I am conscious of the need to support the dynamism of language and that we continue to use a range of language and not limit ourselves and the children to a set of phrases which can become over used, possibly trite, and limiting.

One of the consequences was that, if the teachers did not provide a range of words closely associated with the action in the story, the more general words ran the risk of becoming a chorus, and lost some of their situated meaning. In this project, strategies that worked well for thoughtful conversations, and those strategies that did not, are discussed elsewhere (Carr, 2011). Well-practised shared interactions can set up three features of learner agency that are central to the construction of learner identity: recognition of interest and expertise, co-authoring the learning, and self-assessment. In each of these, there are several ways in which Learning Stories can be a mediating artifact, or 'prop'.[1] They provide opportunities for learners to revisit stories about learning in which they are the 'heroes' and to write or dictate their own story, often using photographs taken of the event as cues. They also provide opportunities for teachers to write stories addressed to the child or children as if in dialogue with them, and sometimes to write the dialogue itself, as Nikki did in Diana's karate story in the previous chapter. We will include examples of each of these.

A story in a portfolio does not, on its own, do the pedagogical work. It must be associated with action of some sort. Sometimes reading-and-writing students writing their own story is that action: the student has reflected on the learning and on the best way of describing it. An example of this is the *Cross Country* story (Learning Story 3.1), written by Michael: 'I felt like I was going to die because I couldn't breathe.' This story format also invites the learner to add a comment in the section 'So what does this mean for my learning in the future?' and Michael adds 'JUST DO IT. NO PAIN, NO GAIN. Use more power up the hill.' And the teacher adds a hand-written comment: 'Pacing yourself is good – You should do that in other situations – maths testing etc.' In this case, planning the way forward was a collaborative task.

Learning Story			
Name: Michael		Date: 31 March	
Activity/Topic: Cross Country		Teacher: Mrs Stimpson	

Child Goals		Indicators	I did my PERSONAL BEST at the x-country by keeping going even when it was difficult. I persevered with the task and did not give up. I was resilient by being smart and pacing myself. I felt like I was going to die because I couldn't breathe. Managed myself by eating a healthy breakfast that had energy and fibre.
Values	Key competencies		
Honesty	**COMMUNICATOR** Using Language, Symbols & Text	· Effectively use communication tools · Share and respond · Numerate and literate · Make positive contributions	
Personal Best	**RESILIENT LEARNER** Managing Self	· Independent · Persevere with tasks · Give new situations a go · Have confidence	
Curiosity	**THINKER** Thinking	· Ask questions - seek answers · Critical and creative thinkers · Organised and plan · Learn from mistakes	
Respect	**CARING CITIZEN** Relating to Others Participating & Contributing	· Co-operate · Participate and contribute positively · Respect others' ideas and beliefs · Take responsibility	

So what does this mean for my learning in the future? JUST DO IT NO PAIN, NO GAIN Use more power up the hill.
Principal Comment: Pacing yourself is good - You should do that in other situations - maths testing etc.

Learning Story 3.1   Cross Country

Recognition of Interest and Expertise

During the 1990s, Mihaly Csikszentmihalyi and his students at the University of Chicago videotaped interviews with a group of 91 'exceptional' individuals, including 14 Nobel Prize winners. They were especially interested in creativity.

Csikszentmihalyi (1996) comments that 'while these people may not have been precocious in their achievements' in their early years, 'they seem to have become committed early to the exploration and discovery of some part of their world' (p. 158). He has this to say about what features of their early years shaped their creative lives:

> According to this view, a creative life is still determined, but what determines it is a will moving across time, the fierce determination to succeed, to make sense of the world, to use whatever means to unravel some of the mysteries of the universe. ... So where does this fierce determination, this unquenchable curiosity come from? Perhaps that question is too reductionistic to be useful. ... It may not be so important to know precisely where the seeds come from. What *is* important is to recognize the interest when it shows itself, nurture it, and provide the opportunities for it to grow into a creative life. (p. 182)

We include here examples from Zeb, a four-year-old who became interested in fish. The data on Zeb comes from the two-year *Learning Wisdom* action research project that focused on 'revisiting' learning. The affordance network (the props) for Zeb's developing interest included qualified teachers, books, charts and websites, photographs of the children's learning activities, learning stories and portfolios. And fish. The fish (several species) and parts of fish were brought into the classroom by teachers and parents over several weeks and a table at the centre was allocated for their exploration. The children were invited to 'get to know' the fish. The teachers noticed, recognised and responded to the children's apparent interest, asked clarifying and probing questions, and made conversational contributions. They took photographs, wrote Learning Stories, recorded the dialogue as they revisited the photographs and the stories, and kept reflective journals. The quote at the beginning of the chapter is from one of the teacher's reflective journals. Box 3.2 is an excerpt from a dialogue as teacher and four-year-old engage in a discussion about his portfolio.

Box 3.2

Zeb's portfolio starts a conversation

An excerpt from a conversation between Zeb and a teacher as they review his portfolio together. Zeb took the lead in a project on fish; in this exchange his meaning-making includes personalising the experiences at the kindergarten: adding emotional intensity by commenting on the fearful and the dangerous, and making connections to information he has remembered (about alligators).

Zeb: And, and I didn't want to touch the, the teeth, 'cos we, 'cos I don't know what dead teeth would feel like. ... I touch my own teeth.

Jackie: Aah. Didn't you touch the shark's teeth?

Z: No, 'cos I think that he could bite.
J: Could bite?
Z: Yeah, but baby ones can just bite you and then they let you go.
J: Do they?
Z: Well alligators bite, they doesn't let you go. ... Because the alligators don't know what they should do, they will eat the kids and they don't eat the adults.

In another conversation, Box 3.3, Zeb watched some photographs on a slide show and then dictated a commentary for his portfolio.

Box 3.3

Excerpts from a conversation as Zeb dictates a commentary for his portfolio

Z: That was my hammerhead shark. That was the shark day. We drawed lots of pictures of sharks and I drawed a volcano that just blew up and it went into the sea and killed a shark. The ash went into the sea and killed a shark.

Z: That's me touching the sharks with my Bob the Builder shirt on.

Z: Hey, what's that one called? A bluenose and my Mum was silly 'cos she thought it was a blue cod. ... And I was right...

Z: ... I didn't want to pick it up because there was blood leaking from it, I just want to touch the smooth parts not the drippy part.

Z: I touched the eye and there was all black stuff coming out of the eye. I can feel the eye, it's squishy.

Z: I didn't know what the snapper was. What's a snapper? (J: The snapper was the one we found on the chart, wasn't it.)

Z: That's my squid...There's three squidwards. They came from my Dad 'cos he catches stinky stuff and I don't like stinky stuff (J: But you like the fish.) Yeh, that's because they not that stinky. Fishies aren't that stinky but squids are really very stinky. When squids cool down they weren't stinky any more. (J: Ok, ok, when they cool down? Why do you think that was?) Because I thought they were still stinky so the sun cooled them down for me, 'cause they were stinky pooh, pooh.

Z: That's so heavy. This was a marlin. Marlins are kind of swordfishes. They can kill people 'cos they hook through you and out your back and they might kill somebody.

Z: [*A photo of Zeb lifting a large bone*] I'm trying to lift it on my head.

Z: [*An out-of-order photo*] That's the marlin again. ... (J: That was [you] looking inside it; do you remember what you saw inside it?) A hole. Blood, and I touched the blood. (J: Did you?) And I never want to touch my blood. 'Cos if someone poked me with a (?) in my tummy I might die and they might touch me and a person might (?) me and it wouldn't mean I'm dead.

Zeb's capacity for scientific activity is being developed by dialogue. Catherine Eberbach and Keith Crowley (2009: 39) state that: 'Fundamental to all scientific activity, expert observation is a complex practice that requires the coordination of disciplinary knowledge, theory, and habits of attention.'[2] Zeb may be developing some of the strategies of expert observation. His *knowledge* about fish is developing as he reviews the photographs, discusses them with the teachers, uses a chart as a source of information: recognising, categorising and characterising. In one of the photos Zeb had climbed up on a table to measure the length of the marlin's spike against his body. His developing capacity for *theorising* includes storying (stories about consequences: sharks and alligators, the volcano that just blew up and the ash that killed the shark), comparison (squids are stinky, fish are not), and his use of the word 'because' or "cos' – ten times in these conversations to refer to causes and consequences. The teacher occasionally directs his *attention*: reminding him that there was a chart to provide information, and asking him 'Do you remember what you saw inside?' He is prepared to admit that he doesn't know ('What's a snapper?'). Some of these comments on the photographs were included in a Learning Story about a marlin swordfish in which Yvonne M., another teacher at this early childhood centre, adds a reminder that they did a bit of research on the Internet because everyone was asking so many questions about swordfish.

This interest and developing expertise in artifacts (objects, languages, storylines), activities (cultural and social practices), or social communities was illustrated in Chapter 3 of the 2001 Book on Learning Stories, where the early research on interest by Suzanne Hidi, Ann Renninger and Andreas Krapp (1992) was referenced. Keith Crowley and Melanie Jacobs (2002) have introduced the idea of 'islands of expertise': topics in which children happen to become interested and in which they develop a relatively deep and rich knowledge. Writing about the role of families in recognising and developing the interests of their preschoolers, especially through visits to museums, they argue that 'islands of expertise become platforms for families to practice learning habits and to develop, often for the first time, conversations about abstract and general ideas, concepts, or mechanisms'(p. 334). So too can islands of expertise become platforms for *classrooms and early childhood centres* to practise learning habits and theories. Csikszentmihalyi (1996) is saying something similar:

> Without a good dose of curiosity, wonder and interest in the way things are like and in how they work, it is difficult to recognize an interesting problem. Openness to experience, a fluid attention that constantly processes events in the environment, is a great advantage for recognising potential novelty. Every creative person is more than amply endowed with these traits. (p. 53)

An open-ended and permeable curriculum can encourage the development of this expertise. Brigid Barron (2006) writes about 'interest and self-sustained

The Big Big Bigger Fish

March
By Yvonne

Zeb, as we have seen on many different occasions, you have been intrigued with all the different types of fish and sea creatures we have had the opportunity to explore at kindy recently. Today you had another opportunity to get up close and touch, smell and explore a huge Marlin swordfish that Tarryn's dad brought in to kindy.

"It's nearly bigger than me."

"They can kill people cos they hook through you and out your back and they might kill somebody."

Zeb, I think you spent nearly the whole session at the table; touching, feeling, opening the mouth, picking up the tail, touching the eyes, gills and fins, and investigating. You were really fascinated with this huge fish head and tail. You were really keen to be involved in the group discussion and share your knowledge. You were quick to identify this fish on our fish chart.

"I can feel its eye, it's squishy."

"It's so heavy, but I can lift this. I'm trying to lift it on my head."

"I know Marlins are kind of swordfishes."

(Continued)

(Continued)

Everyone was asking so many questions so we did a bit of research on the internet.

We found out it can swim reaching speeds of 110kms per hour. We talked about how fast this fish could swim and we decided that it was faster than a car on the motorway. You and Carson had a debate about whether it was faster than a police car!

Once again, Zeb, you really enjoyed today's investigation into this huge fish. You were totally involved and a leader of the group of children, all exploring and working together to discover what they were interested in about the fish.

What I discovered about Zeb today
Zeb, over recent weeks I have noticed that you are intrigued by and have a genuine interest in fish and you have spent a lot of time exploring and investigating the different varieties of fish we have had at kindy. I think that you relished the opportunity today to contribute to our learning programme and share your knowledge and experiences. You love to have huge conversations with the teachers and have your say. I love the confidence you have in your own ability and knowledge and that you are so keen to share this knowledge and confidence with those around you.

Learning Story 3.2   The Big Big Bigger Fish

learning as catalysts of development' and uses the data from three case studies of adolescent learners to argue for an ecological position: ongoing *activities* can spark and sustain an interest; once interest is sparked, people *develop and create learning opportunities* to further their knowledge if they have the time, freedom and resources to learn.

Barron also concludes, as did Crowley and Jacobs, that learning activities based on interests are particularly likely to *cross boundaries* from one place to another (see Chapter 4). An assessment practice that employs Learning Stories and portfolios to document ongoing activities provides opportunities to sustain the interest (for instance, by revisiting episodes of learning), cross the boundaries from place to place and celebrate the growing interest that will make a contribution towards the development of connected islands of expertise. In Chapter 5 we will call these connections 'significant chains of episodes'.

Co-authoring the Learning

At another centre, in a *Transition to School* project, a conversation a few months before Cree was going to leave the early childhood centre to go to school illustrates that children's ideas are taken seriously. Cree and Jemma (one of the teachers) were reviewing Cree's portfolio together. Jemma reports on this conversation and its consequences in a Learning Story entitled 'Maybe Music?':

We looked at all the stories detailing her learning. I (Jemma) asked her if she felt there was anything else she would like to have included. 'I'll have to have a think about it'. After a few minutes (thinking) she replied 'I have an idea. Maybe music?'. After a discussion she said she would like a CD of her favourite songs from kindergarten. I suggested we make a list of her favourite songs. 'But how can I do that when I don't know how to write the words, and I can't read them' she exclaimed. 'I know', she quickly answered herself, 'Why don't I listen to the songs and then I can tell you which ones I like and then you can write it down' Great idea Cree, and that's just what we did. [The other teachers added that they were going to do this for every child.] (Hartley, Rogers, Smith, Peters and Carr, forthcoming, Chapter 9)

As in the example with Zeb, photographs have often been the centre of focus for reciprocal conversations. Marianne, a teacher whose comment about developing a 'shared history of knowledge' with one of the children is included in Chapter 1, commented in her reflective journal that 'Writing the [learning] story with the child as the child tells the story, with a few key questions, supports capturing the child's view and dialogical thinking.' In Learning Story 3.3, Emma dictated a story from photographs of her block construction.

Some of the features of narrative quality as listed by Reese, Suggate and Lang (2010) in Chapter 2 (p.32) are in this narrative: temporal, causal and locative information. *Temporal information*: I started off with, but then I recognised, so then I, this gave me ideas for. *Causal information*: But then I recognised, so then I; the volcano exploded because there were too many cars and roads; the earthquake moved the ground and that's why the cars got broken. *Locative information:* In the books are volcanos that look like real ones. This gave me ideas for building my volcano. Jerome Bruner (2002: 34) outlines some key features of narrative quality as well. He quotes Kenneth Burke (1945) to suggest that, at a minimum, a story (fictional or actual) requires 'an Agent who performs an Action to achieve a Goal in a recognizable Setting by the use of certain Means. What drives the story is a misfit between some of the elements of the Pentad: Trouble.' Perhaps there are two Agents here in Emma's story: herself the builder and the Volcano. It is the Volcano that causes the drama and the Trouble ('Some of the blocks fall down when the volcano explode. It's just exploded'; 'My volcano earthquaked when it erupted'). Bruner comments that 'Interest in narrative has grown steadily in the last decade or two, particularly in the power of the story form to shape our conceptions of reality and legitimacy' (2002: 111).

Writing about research on *collaboration* as a conceptual and dispositional strategy, Melissa Gresalfi (2009) comments that:

(G)roups in which students ask for help, challenge one another, and provide support create opportunities for all students to engage more deeply with content. … In particular, these behaviors allow students to take on more responsibility for making meaning. … The act of explaining and justifying their ideas helps students to become attuned to the opportunities to make connections between ideas. (p. 262–3)

My Volcano

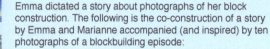

Emma dictated a story about photographs of her block construction. The following is the co-construction of a story by Emma and Marianne accompanied (and inspired) by ten photographs of a blockbuilding episode:

My volcano is big. Some of the blocks fall down when the volcano explodes. It's just exploded. Janet helped me because she got a book out for me about volcanoes. Avalon and Lucy were also building this volcano. I started off with square blocks but then I recognised that volcanos are supposed to be round, so then I put the round blocks on the bottom and the long blocks inside the round blocks. I built towers and roads amongst the volcano. In the books are volcanos that look like real ones. This gave me ideas for building my volcano with Avalon and Lucy. My volcano earthquaked when it erupted. The cars and the road got all broken when the volcano exploded and the earthquake moved the ground.
The volcano exploded because there were too many cars and roads. The earthquake moved the ground and that's why the cars got broken. The red blocks were the lava inside of the volcano.

What learning is happening here?

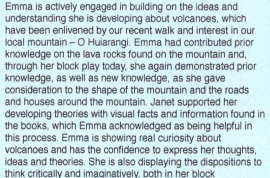

Emma is actively engaged in building on the ideas and understanding she is developing about volcanoes, which have been enlivened by our recent walk and interest in our local mountain – O Huiarangi. Emma had contributed prior knowledge on the lava rocks found on the mountain and, through her block play today, she again demonstrated prior knowledge, as well as new knowledge, as she gave consideration to the shape of the mountain and the roads and houses around the mountain. Janet supported her developing theories with visual facts and information found in the books, which Emma acknowledged as being helpful in this process. Emma is showing real curiosity about volcanoes and has the confidence to express her thoughts, ideas and theories. She is also displaying the dispositions to think critically and imaginatively, both in her block construction and with the story she shared today.

31st May By Marianne

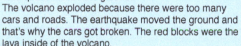

She writes that a facilitating environment is one in which students are 'expected, obligated and entitled to explain' (p. 363). In another group block-building story (see Learning Story 3.4), this time from the north of England, *Ilaria, Isabella and Katharine's Learning Story*, Isabella's parent added the comment that she 'was able to explain what she had done to make the construction strong'.

In Yvonne S.'s Learning Story in Chapter 1, Abagail was expected and entitled to explain, and Zeb's conversation of scientific meaning-making illustrated this as well. Zeb's use of 'because' in his retelling was an example of explaining and justifying; Emma's retelling also includes explaining and justifying her ideas for an interested listener who was not there at the time ('I started off with square blocks but then I recognised that volcanos are supposed to be round, so then I put the round blocks on the bottom and the long blocks inside the round blocks'. 'The red blocks were the lava'), and an acknowledgement of the assistance that she received from a teacher and two other children. Like Zeb, but at a different centre, a volcano is the agent that provides Trouble, in Emma's case for the cars, in Zeb's case for the shark. For Emma, a story line was first created in a block construction and for Zeb a shark story was first told in a drawing. Similarly, a drawing provided the impetus for a story entitled *Illustrator, Author and Publisher* (Learning Story 3.5), dictated by Thenusan. The Learning Story begins: 'Today I discovered Thenusan at the drawing table. Thenusan explained he was drawing a snake. A snake, very interesting! Iggy and Connor were working on their drawing designs of monster trucks. Thenusan was listening to their stories and decided to add a monster truck to his design too. I offered to write Thenusan's story.' Karen R. writes the story as dictated by the author, then she and Thenusan turn it into a book and it is read to the children at 'mat-time' at the end of the morning. Thenusan began attending kindergarten 18 months prior to this Learning Story. At the time he started he spoke no English.

Self-assessment

As we have become more convinced of the value for long-term learning of learners developing a capacity for self-assessment, so teachers have found a number of ways in which children can be involved in narrative assessments in ways that can be construed as self-assessment: revisiting photographs and stories, writing or dictating the story, and stories addressed to the learner. In a Learning Story from the same classroom as Michael's *Cross Country* story, Thomas has written a Learning Story about his costume-making. In a section labelled 'What does this mean for my learning in the future?' he writes: 'I learned it was important to learn from my mistakes. I accidentally cut the sleeves of the first top I made, so I had to make it again. When I made the next top I was really careful about how I cut it. I will keep trying.' A handwritten

Ilaria, Isabella and Katharine's Learning Story
written by Nichola

We have been reading stories about Percy the Park Keeper and you decided to make a home for the woodland animals. I really enjoyed watching your tree-house spread and grow. You thought carefully about building a place for all the different types of animals. You worked very well together, each building a part of the giant tree-house. You even remembered to build a high place for the owls to sit.

You chose the bricks that you used very carefully, to make sure you built a tree-house that didn't fall down.

What learning is happening here?
Ilaria, Isabella and Katharine worked very well together, spending time making improvements to their building.
They had an excellent use of descriptive language and were able to introduce a storyline into their play.

Opportunities and Possibilities
Ilaria, Isabella and Katharine are enjoying reading stories about Percy the Park Keeper and learning about the different environments that animals live in. We will continue to look at the types of environments that woodland animals live in and provide opportunities in the sand for Ilaria, Isabella and Katharine to create an environment.

Parent comments
Isabella told me she really enjoyed making this home and was able to explain what she had done to make the construction strong.

Learning Story 3.4   Ilaria, Isabella and Katharine's Learning Story

Illustrator, Author and Publisher!

Today I discovered Thenusan at the drawing table. Thenusan explained he was drawing a snake.

A snake, how interesting! Iggy and Connor were working on their drawing designs of monster trucks. Thenusan was listening to their stories and decided to add a monster truck to his design too.

I offered to write Thenusan's story.

Here it is...........

The snake is catching the monster truck. The monster truck run away. The snake followed the monster truck. The monster truck goes down. The snake gets up on the road.
Next the snake goes where the truck is and catches it. Snake is going up and the snake is flying up into the clouds. The snake eats the monster truck and goes inside the snake.
The snake is stuck and next the tiger eats the snake.
Next the lion eats the snake.
Giraffe is eating the grass. The giraffe was drinking water.
The zebra is eating grass. The zebra is drinking water and eating mud. Next it is drinking muddy water and it is running away from the zoo. Somebody was watching TV next the zebra was running in the house. It was going to break the house and next the house fell down. The people fell down in the house. Next the zebra is going to the zoo.
The spider is eating the banana. Next the spider is going to drink the water. Next the spider is going to the mummy. Next the spider is going to the mummy. Next the spider is going to the daddy. The sunset and you can't go there.

WOW! What an interesting story! I suggested Thenusan may like to think about turning his story into a book and he could draw illustrations of the other characters. Thenusan was keen to continue work and set about creating the next page.

Thenusan was a little unsure about how to draw a giraffe, so we collected a figure from the zoo corner and Thenusan used this as a model. Work continued and before long Thenusan had completed all the illustrations.

(Continued)

(Continued)

I typed Thenusan's story out (there were so many words to fit on the first page) and Thenusan glued each paragraph in place. Now it was off to the laminator and book binder to construct the book. Thenusan laminated the pages together and then crunched the holes in the edges to create a spine for his book.

Thenusan's book was the first book read at mat time today and Thenusan shared his story with all of his friends.

What learning do I think is happening for Thenusan?

Thenusan is a highly motivated, self-directed learner, who sets his own tasks. Thenusan's picture is amazing and it is clear to see he spent time working on it. He was very focused on his work and persisted with the task until he had completed his design. We have noticed Thenusan's spoken English going from strength to strength and he is very keen to share and express his ideas about his work. When Thenusan began his story telling today he developed his ideas and this created a more complex story.

Thenusan took on the role of Illustrator, Author and finally Publisher, when he turned his pages into a book. Using technology (the laminator and book binder) in an integrated way is providing a meaningful early literacy experience for Thenusan. The last act of the day was to use Thenusan's story book as our story for our mat time. Yes, presenter comes to mind as Thenusan shared his story with all of our whānau.

Thenusan knows text has a purpose (to record and read) and today we wrote down his ideas. The first copy was a draft and the second copy was printed from the computer. Through the story telling process, Thenusan is developing his creative thinking and formulating his ideas.

Thenusan's passion for exploring in the outdoors, and in particular tree-climbing, has directly supported his journey into drawing, story telling and writing. We know it is wise practice for children to have many opportunities to engage in outdoor activities, such as climbing, swinging and running. Bush Kindergarten has provided many possibilities for Thenusan to explore and it seems to me this has directly influenced his learning in the 'normal' kindergarten environment.

11th October Karen

Here are the pages that make up Thenusan's book.

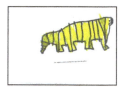

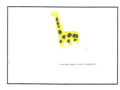

Learning Story 3.5   Illustrator, Author and Publisher!

parent comment says, 'We could tell by the costumes that the group worked well together while making them. They were perfect to help tell the story about Maui and the Fish.' In Box 3.4, a younger learner, Zac, is highlighting his new competence and explaining the role of observation and imitation in learning.

Box 3.4

In one early childhood centre Delwyn (the teacher) is revisiting his portfolio with Zac, and they discuss a story in which Zac has drawn a STOP sign for the road play. Zac makes a connection with his earlier observation of a 'workman' and reminds Delwyn why he is 'clever':

Zac:	I drawed that! It means Stop. (He is referring to a very large STOP sign he had written for the road play one day. We made it into a sign. Zac had copied my letters from a small piece of paper)
Delwyn:	How did you learn to write those letters?
Z:	I clever. I learned that by myself – because I saw a workman doing that so I thought I could do it.

A story from England entitled *The Genius* (see Learning Story 3.6) opens with the comment:

> Toby, I looked across from the snack table today and heard you shout 'I've done it, I've done it, I'm a genius!'. I came over to find out exactly what you had done that had made you so excited. ... I watched as you expertly used the screw driver to remove the tiny screws around the circuit board. I was amazed at the skill and strength that you showed with the tools, and your determination to take the computer apart.

The self-assessment is Toby's, and in this case the teacher provides a 'split-screen' analysis to remind him of his technology skills and his determination. She comments on the way in which he can now use 'real tools with expert skill', and invokes a 'rotation' schema to describe his interest. Toby describes himself as 'a genius in my head and a genius in my hands', reminiscent of the way in which Zeb, Emma and Thenusan made a drawing or a block construction before they could tell a story.

Jigsaws provide feedback on achievements, enabling children to self-assess without the need for praise or explanation of the skills and determination by the teacher. A story about Angel (see Learning Story 3.7) describes her assistance to another child and the ways in which she had increased the challenge: seeking out more and more difficult tasks. This is an example, too, of a short story that covers episodes of increasing challenge and success over three different days. Another story from the Lady Gowrie Centre in Adelaide in which the playground equipment does the assessing and the learner supplies the determination is illustrated in *See What I Can Do* (see Learning Story 3.8).

The Genius

Toby, I looked across from the snack table today and heard you shout, "I've done it, I've done it, I'm a genius!" I came over to find out exactly what you had done that had made you so excited. You had a screwdriver in your hand, and had just added another screw to the pot that you held. I was aware that you had been deeply involved in taking apart Mrs Brown's old computer, and had been working on it for a considerable time. I watched as you expertly used the screwdriver to remove the tiny screws around the circuit board. I was amazed at the skill and strength that you showed with the tools, and your determination to take the computer apart. I remembered, Toby, that I had often seen you turning or rotating objects, and had thought that this was a pattern or schema in your play. You have practiced and refined your skills of turning, Toby, and are now quite an expert!

I told you how impressed I was and you replied, "I'm a genius in my head and a genius in my hands!" I agreed that you certainly were a genius at taking apart computers! Later, when we told the class about your skills, you explained that you had discovered what was wrong with Mrs Brown's computer – a connecting lead had come off – and that you knew exactly how to fix it. You decided that you would sort it out for her tomorrow!

What have I learnt about Toby today?

I have learnt such a lot about Toby today! His high level of involvement really amazed me! I could see concentration, energy, complexity and satisfaction, which made me realise that Toby is involved in deep level learning. Rotation schema has been something that Toby has explored over time, and I can now see that Toby has refined his physical skills so much that he can use real tools with expert skill. He has gained understanding of how to twist, turn, do up and undo things, and has a real interest in 'what's inside'. Toby is asking questions and solving problems for himself. I have also learnt that Toby has gained in confidence, and now sees himself as 'a genius' who is prepared to 'have a go' and face learning challenges.

Opportunities and Possibilities

I wonder if Mummy and Daddy have noticed Toby's new skills and confidence at home? What is Toby a 'genius' at there? I can't wait to join Toby again and see where his exploration of 'rotation' will take us. Perhaps we could use some other tools and find out what's inside something else?

Nicola, September

Learning Story 3.6   The Genius

Children are learning the language of valued learning and putting it to use. A story written by Jacqui, about two children *Building a Sticky Bridge* from cellotape (see Learning Story 3.9), is placed in each of their portfolios. It is personalised in two places. Attached is Elizabeth's version. Elizabeth had explained

Angel - March, By Helen

Angel, as you and Nehu were finishing this pirate ship puzzle together the other day, you excitedly told me how you had helped Nehu fit the pieces together correctly. You must have seen this large puzzle as a challenge because you set yourself a goal, which was to complete it all by yourself, and that is just what you did!

The next day you asked me to get the puzzle out for you and you did it again by yourself. To make it more challenging, you set yourself another goal, which was to do it without using the picture on the box as a guide, and again, you did it. The following day, you came with me to the storeroom to seek out some more large puzzles to create more challenges for yourself.

Short term review:

Angel, you have really enjoyed doing our large puzzles and experienced the satisfaction of completing them all by yourself. Along the way, you set yourself goals and successfully achieved them - tino pai Angel!

Learning Story 3.7 "I Can Do It!"

to the teacher how she and Lucy were working together, and she referred to a wall display of cooperative ventures to ask the teacher what label was used for 'working together' on the wall display. The teacher noted, 'I said it was called collaboration, so you went back to tell Lucy that you were collaborating with her!' It became clear that this word had some agency for Elizabeth, when her mother told a follow-on story of Grandad's concern that using six rolls of cellotape to build a bridge was a bit of a waste of cellotape. Jacqui comments to Elizabeth in the story that: 'Mum said that you told him that "Jacqui didn't call it wasting when you were collaborating and being creative."'

Concluding Comments

A number of processes of agency and dialogue as part of an assessment were in action here: using the portfolio as a catalyst to have a shared conversation (Zeb); teaching others (*I Can Do It*); learning the vocabulary of learning (*Building a Sticky Bridge*); dictating a story and reading the story to the class (*Illustrator, Author and Publisher*); and dictating the Learning Story or re-telling a story inspired by the Learning Story (Zeb and Emma). Pamela Moss (2008) has commented on the relationship between giving some of the authorship to the learner in assessment practices and the development of positional identities.

See what I can do!

Dear Mum and Dad,

Today Kit discovered the climbing in Kurrajong. Kit, you climbed up the ramp on your hands and knees –

> and I was absolutely thrilled to see you reach the top. Once at the top you decided to climb over the red frame onto the ramp on the other side.

You stretched your hand out to reach the red frame, you had to try a few times and it was really tricky balancing yourself.

> But you did it! You looked up at Steph and Erin, who were sitting close by to celebrate with you! You were so proud of what you had done.

Next, you moved your leg off the ramp, over the red frame. Steph came and sat with you and helped you when you called out, "My leg's stuck!"

Then you had to move your other leg over the red frame and onto the plank. Steph was behind you, talking to you about what you were doing as you climbed.

> Once your leg was over, you stretched out your arm and put your hand down on the plank. You looked back at Steph to ask for help; you were finding it hard to stay balanced.

With Steph's help, you finally had two hands on the plank and you pulled your whole body over the red frame and down onto the ramp.

> Finally, you slid off the side of the ramp and beamed a smile to Erin and Steph as if to say 'I made it!'

(Continued)

(Continued)

What does this mean for Kit?

From this experience, we can see that Kit is exploring her environment thoroughly. She spends time at each experience, determined to fulfil her ideas in that space. Kit is challenging herself, making attempts to complete each step, asking for help from me when she needs it. Kit is also learning about her body, the way it moves, bends and stretches, manipulating her movements to reach the next step.

What's next for Kit?

In order to support Kit's developing interest in her environment, I will provide her with opportunities to discover new spaces and experiences. I will be with Kit in moments of discovery, talking with her about what she has found or achieved, as well as talking with her about challenges, and stepping in to offer support when she needs it. Finally, I will be with Kit and will share her delight in what she has done.

By Stephanie, April

Learning Story 3.8   See What I Can Do!

She warns that students will learn 'to act with the kinds of agency they are afforded when they are assessed' (p. 239). Michael, Zeb, Emma, Cree, Isabella, Thenusan, Zac, Toby, Angel, Kit and Lucy, in this chapter, were being assessed with exactly the kinds of agency that the everyday programme was affording them: a democratic sharing of ideas.

Neil Mercer (2002) has written from his research on how teachers use language as 'the principal tool of their trade' (p. 143), and his conclusions are relevant to the discussion in this chapter:

> We concluded that the quality of children's educational experience is significantly affected by the extent to which their dialogue with the teacher gives what they are doing in class a continuity of meaning (so that activity is contextualized by the history of past experience) and a comprehensible and worthwhile purpose. (p. 145)

On the significant role that dialogue plays in learning, Mercer wrote: 'We need ways of describing how intersubjectivity (in the sociocultural sense of this term used by Wertsch, 1984) is pursued, maintained, or lost in the course of classroom talk' (2008: 38). Mercer and Karen Littleton (2007) have more to say about 'intersubjectivity': the notion that teaching and learning interactions 'are exercises in collectivity, involving both the child and the adult in processes of negotiation, disagreement, the exchange and sharing of information, judgement, decision-making and evaluation of one another's contributions' (p. 22).

BUILDING A STICKY BRIDGE

Written by Jacqui - 25th November

Today, you and Lucy were very busy working in the collage area. You had the great idea of making a bridge with cellotape and were working with tremendous concentration to put this plan into action. Your bridge began to look like one of the pictures I had seen in my new bridge book, so I brought it to show you. You guys are great engineers!

What might Elizabeth be learning in this Story?
You and Lucy work together so well, Elizabeth; I am really impressed by the way you share ideas with each other and negotiate. You are also a respectful and generous friend – you were very quick to tell everyone that the bridge had been "Lucy's idea in the first place". Did you realize that you worked together for two and a half hours making this bridge? You have an amazing ability to focus and concentrate on your projects.
When you came to talk to me about how you were working together, you asked what it was called in our wall display; I said it was called collaboration, so you went back to tell Lucy that you were collaborating with her! You really like words don't you? I'll tell you a secret, I love words too!

Opportunities and Possibilities
The challenges that you set for yourselves are just so much bigger than I could set. I think I will just wait and watch and get ready to be impressed when your next fantastic creative idea is being worked on.

Parent Response:
Mum told me that when you brought this story home, Grandad was visiting your house. He was worried that using six rolls of cellotape to build a bridge was a bit of a waste of cellotape. But Mum said that you told him that, "Jacqui didn't call it wasting when you were collaborating and being creative." Your Mum was really impressed that you were able to use those words and defend your use of building materials! So am I!

Learning Story 3.9   Building a Sticky Bridge

In the examples in this chapter these shared interactions could be maintained when the teachers took photographs of the children's learning, wrote Learning Stories for their portfolios, revisited those photographs and stories with them, listened to their views, and added their own. These ideas about agency and dialogue are just as relevant for interactions between families and teachers, as the provision at Pen Green in Northamptonshire has illustrated (Whalley and the Pen Green Centre Team, 2001). As we will see in Chapter 4, when interesting stories cross the border from the early childhood centre into the school classroom and into the home, they construct opportunities for continuing these conversations in another place.

Notes

1   In the New Zealand national Early Childhood Curriculum, Te Whāriki, one of the principles of the curriculum is described as 'Children learn through responsive and reciprocal relationships with people, places and things.' Bronwen Cowie, in a search for another 'P' word has suggested that the affordance network could be described as 'people, places and props' (personal communication, February 2011). This sits nicely with the theme of this chapter – authoring – with an implicit theatre metaphor. Bruner's definition of a 'good' story is one that contains actors, scenes, plot and Trouble. In the *Learning in the making* book (Carr, Smith, Duncan, Jones, Lee and Marshall, 2010) we also employ this metaphor to suggest:

>   that the children in this study were developing self-scripts for learning. These 'scripts' for a multifaceted learner self were about what learners do and might assume, and what opportunities to look out for. (pp. 196–7)

2   See also Tom Rice (2010). In a very different context, Rice is writing about two of the ideas in this chapter: dispositions and agency. He uses Pierre Bourdieu's work, describes key dispositions for a doctor 'habitus', and writes about the way in which agency is sited in the relationship between student doctors and their stethoscopes. It is worthwhile contemplating that for some of these children, the 'hallmark' of a learner is sited in their Learning Story portfolio, and their use of it as a mediating tool in their relationships with others. Carol Hartley, Pat Rogers, Jemma Smith, Sally Peters and Margaret Carr, writing about five-year-old Gaurav's portfolio as an affordance for communication and relationships in his first year of school, say that he 'used it to engage children in conversation, sharing his ideas and recalling previous experiences. … He used it to introduce himself to other new children as they started. Quite soon a number of children were bringing their "kindy books" to school and there were several observations of other children using these to foster relationships' (forthcoming).

Making Connections Across Boundaries Between Places

Box 4.1

Family and friends. Yeah. When my grandad was sick in hospital they would take it to him and show him what they had been doing at kindy. Just anyone who comes over, they love to show it: 'Look what I have been doing at kindy'… Louis is not really interested in books but he will read his portfolio and he's starting to read more books and wanting us to read him more books. … So I think maybe his bedtime was, he never wanted to read a story, he would rather watch a DVD or just go to sleep; but reading his portfolio, he would rather read that because he knows what the story is going to say because he is in it. (Interview with four-year-old Kellen and three-year-old Louis's mother, Kylee, asked about the portfolios at home)

We introduced the notion of assessments as 'boundary objects' in Chapter 1, and in that chapter we also quoted Etienne Wenger's (1998) comment that identity is a matter of 'straddling across boundaries and finding ways of being in the world that can encompass multiple, conflicting perspectives in the course of addressing significant issues' (pp. 274–5). Wenger adds that this is one of the most critical aspects of education for the kind of world we live in, and we agree. The world we live in is a different world from the one in which we and our forebears grew up, hence the discussion in Chapter 1 about strengthening horizontal connections as we build on the vertical legacy from previous generations. Learning Stories and portfolios physically cross boundaries, and the ideas in them do too. They can begin conversations with families about their children's learning, provide opportunities to connect the children's learning in the classroom or the early childhood centre to their lives (and selves) in other places, and make connections with the wider community outside the centre or classroom.

Kellen shares his portfolio with younger sister Peyton. Peyton was finding all the pictures that she and her dad appeared in.

Conversations with Families about their Children's Learning

In Chapter 1 we cited the synthesis of research by John Hattie, which concluded that parental expectations are far more powerful influences on children's learning than many of the structural features of the home. Just as Learning Stories have provided something interesting to talk about with children, as we saw in Chapter 3, they also provide something interesting to talk about with families as well, and these conversations are often about expectations for their children. The implications for children's learning of boundaries between home and school are a key theme of Liz Brooker's book *Starting school: Young children learning cultures* (2002) about the experience of 16 four-year-olds who started school in the same reception class in England. She comments on the boundary effects between home and school:

> The boundaries take many forms, and their effect tends to be cumulative: children who were disadvantaged through one form of boundary maintenance (such as transfer of information about the child from home to school) tend to be disadvantaged in other respects (such as frequency of home-school reading activity). ... Children who are cut off from their home and family when they start school have less chance of creating all the links necessary for such [secure and reciprocal] relationships, or of fully assimilating the school ethos. (p. 163)

Norma González, Luis Moll and Cathy Amanti's 2005 edited book on *Funds of knowledge: Theorizing practices in households, communities, and classrooms* describes a number of projects designed to make visible in school the knowledges from the families and homes of Mexican American families. Classroom and home observations and interviews with families researched how families generated, obtained and distributed knowledge, and all the projects emphasised the strengths and resources that families possess. In New Zealand, Stuart McNaughton has researched the ways in which the diversity of family literacy practices can be included in school literacy practices (McNaughton, 2002). Pat Thomson (2002) had coined the phrase 'virtual school bags', and she and Christine Hall (Thomson and Hall, 2008: 89) report that: 'children come to school with virtual school bags of knowledges, experiences and dispositions. However, school only draws on the contents of some children's school bags, those whose resources match those required in the game of education.'

Learning Stories frequently invite contributions from families in writing, and although one would imagine that families who are not confident in their writing ability would be reluctant to contribute, we have not found this to be the case. In a kindergarten receiving additional funding because of its 'vulnerable' status,[1] three features of the portfolios appeared to influence a high level of contribution: the Learning Stories positioned the children as having skills and qualities of value; invitations to the families to contribute were personalised inside the Stories; and portfolios were sent home regularly in a 'school' book bag, paralleling the official school expectation that families would read the stories to their children. Many of the families were familiar with the school book bags from the school experience of older siblings and cousins and the opportunity to enter into a conversation about learning shifted in strength from merely being *available* to being *inviting* and *personalised* (Clarkin-Phillips and Carr, forthcoming). Each time that the portfolio went home, the teachers added an eye-catching invitation to the families to make a comment. Family members responded by writing reciprocal comments from home, and added notes of recognition of the learning at the kindergarten. A comfortable sofa near the bookshelf of portfolios invited revisiting with the children of the Learning Stories and the families' comments.

Box 4.2

Family comments in their child's portfolio in a kindergarten

Ngauru's portfolio. August. Ngauru really enjoys coming to kindy and is really excelling. Thanks to all the teachers.

May in the next year. Ngauru enjoys showing her book to all her whānau, nans, koros, aunties, uncles. Ngauru's whānau are so impressed with all the learning experiences she has had. Thank you.

Ngakau's portfolio. August. The book is awesome. I am glad to see that my son is interacting with other children and learning so much, over the months since Ngakau has been at kindy the family has noticed a big change in Ngakau. Thankyou.

March the next year. As Ngakau and myself read through the book it was nice to hear my son explain things to me with excitement and enthusiasm. I see Ngakau has achieved a lot since he has been at … Kindy interacting with other children and the teachers. Thank you Caryll, Tania and Michelle for opening a whole new world in Ngakau's eyes. His book is beautiful.

Calvin's portfolio. August. Calvin: Daddy says your kindy book is awesome! It is nice to see you being part of a group and playing with your friends. Calvin: Mummy loves looking at your book with you and talking about all the people in your photos. It is neat to see you with your friends in the photos as you often talk about which of your friends you are going to play with.

March the next year (a comment from Calvin). 'It looks flash' Daddy said this about my book. Then mummy took a photo of us reading my book in bed.

Writing about the way in which the notion of 'funds of knowledge' is a rejection of deficit views of communities and families, Thomson and Hall add that: 'The affirmation of home and community practices also builds positive social identities for students and sensitises their teachers to the myriad ways in which the mandated curriculum excludes some and privileges others' (2008: 88). Learning Stories are also a rejection of deficit views of a child's identity as a learner, both at home and at the kindergarten. At Caryll, Tania and Michelle's kindergarten (see Box 4.2) recent Learning Stories were displayed on a board near the entrance to the kindergarten; there was a theme of links to competence and interests at home and in the community. There were, for instance, two stories about George's interest in and knowledge about lawn mowers and his ambition to own one. A photograph added by the teacher is closely inspected by George, and the text adds: 'We looked closely at the picture and you wondered how the catcher at the back would stay on so we talked about whether there would be clips or a special bolt to hold it on.' The teacher adds some comments about how they might build on this interest:

> After I had finished talking with you, I did some thinking about how we could extend your interest, and had an idea that Mr B from [the local] School mows the school lawns on a ride-on mower! George, do you think we should call out to Mr B over the fence and ask him if he can show you the mower, and maybe he may let you sit on it, and look at the controls and we could ask about how the catcher is attached!

A story called 'Janice's Big Trip Up North' tells the story of her recent trip away from the kindergarten, and adds a map. Another story entitled 'Jayden Saves the Day' recounts a story told by Jayden and his mother, when Jayden went into the kitchen and yelled out, 'Mum, Mum your tea towel is burning!'. The teachers also developed for each child a Transition to School portfolio of stories aligned both to the Early Childhood Curriculum strands and to the school Key Competencies; they selected a few recent Learning Stories from the early childhood portfolio to place in this Transition to School portfolio to describe 'readiness for school' in a narrative way.

Resilient families have been found to have beliefs that enable them to affirm and focus on strengths and possibilities (Walsh, 1998). Learning Stories are designed to foreground developing strengths and possibilities, to enable 'learners first to engage with new ways of being and acting associated with new, aspirational identities; and second to have these recognised as legitimate' in the words of John Pryor and Barbara Crossouard (2008: 3), quoted in Chapter 2. A qualitative sub-project of the EPPE longitudinal research by Iram Siraj-Blatchford and colleagues (Siraj-Blatchford, 2010) on how children succeeded at school 'against the odds' found that a contributing factor to this success was a belief that effort made a difference, and that this belief was shared by the child.

Learning Stories are reifying[2] – documenting in ways that travel – the many ways in which 'intelligence' grows with experience. The alternative belief in development as simply the unfolding of natural ability, not uncommonly held by both teachers and families, can impoverish opportunities for education in the early years. Research in neuroscience is beginning to provide additional information about the role of early childhood experiences 'before neural commitment' in the early setting up of inclinations, expectations and interests. In a chapter from the 2006 *Cambridge handbook of the learning sciences*, John Bransford, Brigid Barron, Roy Pea and others, writing about 'learning in infancy before neural commitment' comment that:

> One thing has been established without a doubt – learning experiences help sculpt an individual's brain. Brain development is not a product of biology exclusively, but, more accurately, a complex interaction of both. (p. 22)

Responding to a Learning Story about her fragile young child, a parent commented:

> It is amazing how the smallest thing can be amazing. I was so excited with Kian's story that I went out and bought a bottle of wine to celebrate. I can't tell you how amazing it is to have someone else tell you what your child 'can' do instead of all the 'can'ts'. The processes that the centre uses to encourage Kian to communicate are very good, and since learning these things, I am looking at Kian in a different light and attempting to talk with him rather than at him. (Carr, Lee and Jones, 2004, 9: 22)

In another centre (see Learning Story 4.1), a grandmother sent a story about learning at home to Ash's early childhood centre, describing an interest in patterning at home and wondering if this interest had 'crossed the boundary' into the early childhood centre.[3]

Some families contribute photographs to their children's portfolios, and occasionally their own Learning Stories from home. In a school in Cheshire, Paige's family sent some photographs of their trip to the beach. The teacher asked Paige to comment on the pictures, and wrote it up as a Learning Story (See Box 4.3).

Who did this?

Just thought you'd love this one ...
I arrived home from my walk last night and was greeted by this most perfect arrangement at the front door. "Who did this?" I asked. Well, it seems that Ash was asked to put his shoes away and took the opportunity to tidy up all the shoes lying in the entrance-way. I would like to think this has something to do with a propensity toward tidiness and orderliness. Mmmm, maybe it has more to do with his ever-increasing preoccupation with matching and lining things up. Has he busied himself with things like this at the centre?
14th May from Nana (Jocelyn)

Learning Story 4.1   Who Did This?

Box 4.3

Paige's family trip to the beach

In a Learning Story from a school in Cheshire, Paige brought in some photos of her visit to the beach, and the teacher took photos of her with the photos, and wrote Paige's comments. The comments included 'I was doing my kite with my mum and then my mum had a go after me. I had a little drink in my van and then I went back in the van for a bit to eat, that was after I'd been in the sea.' 'That's when I was building a sand castle with my dad. Look at his hat.' 'When I was by my van it was flying on its own.' (Teacher: What was flying? Paige pointed to the kite string tied to the post.) 'This is the crab's shell but it was the crab's snapper' (opening and closing her finger and thumb).

At the same time as taking the family and the beach into the classroom, Paige is developing an ability to tell a sequential story using *then* and *after*, a feat that needs a high level of concentration. The photographs have assisted her with this. She is also focusing the teacher's attention on key features that are significant for her (Dad's hat) and using a gesture to explain what she means by a 'snapper'. The teacher reminds her to explain an element of the story that may be unclear to an audience ('What was flying?').

In Peetshaya's portfolio, an extended contribution by an older sister includes the comment:

> She shares everything with me that she does in the school. She keeps them in her mind and as soon as I reach home after school she tells me. ... During the night time before going to bed she makes me tell her the stories from the storybooks. She says spell my name then she writes it that's awesome.

Connecting the Children's Learning in the Classroom or the Early Childhood Centre to Their Lives (and Selves) in Other Places

It is common in conversations about learning for children to make references to home, to the people and to their experiences there. Marianne, the teacher whose comments are included in Chapters 1 and 3, noted that, 'Jack shared many stories that had been passed onto him from his family so there was a real sense of connectedness ... Over time, through his sharing [conversations], I got to know different people in his family. I got to know his interests and strengths and that he likes to visit the old days, so we had layers of stories building.'

In the longitudinal study, *Learning in the making*, a chapter on 'storying selves' includes details about the importance of that storying for the families of two of the case study children, Yasin and Aralynn:

> Yasin's conversations with teachers at the kindergarten set out the contexts of a cultural self: the country outside New Zealand, India, where his nana and extended family live, and his family in New Zealand who are widening his perceptions of self as a global citizen by introducing him to new languages – Spanish, Arabic and Mandarin ... By school, however, this cultural self has been left behind. ... For Aralynn, the storying [*about her family*] could continue into school, in a smaller classroom than Yasin's. Her subject-based knowing – her love of, and knowledge about, gardening, which began at home with her mother and grandparents – is also part of the valued school curriculum. (Carr, Smith, Duncan, Jones, Lee and Marshall, 2010: 192–3)

At school, Aralynn seized every opportunity to bring in something interesting from home for News Time. Her classroom teachers commented that she will sometimes be 'the only one that has bothered to bring special or Science Nature news ... she's actually kept to the topic' (ibid.: 191). Learning Stories that include comments about people and events at home can gather together many facets of a young child's identity, for instance as a member of an extended family or a gardener. Other facets appear in the examples from Isabella's and Devya's portfolios (Learning Stories 4.2 and 4.3): for Isabella as a grandchild, jewellery maker, writer and, for Devya, as a writer and a member of a home culture with a long tradition.

An Act of Kindness

It was the very beginning of the day, in fact Isabella had just walked in the door and, after I had greeted her, I asked the question, "I wonder what your plans are for today, Isabella?" In no time Isabella replied, "I am going to make a necklace for my grandma, she is going to hospital."

 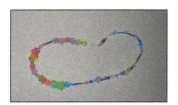 

Isabella set to work. When she had finished threading, I suggested she may like to wrap the necklace and complete her gift by making a card.

Isabella carefully wrapped the necklace and then dictated her message and added the finishing touches – her name, kisses and beautiful pictures.

Dear Grandma,

Is everything good at hospital? I hope you have a nice time there and I think everything is o.k.
I hope you have a nice operation and I hope you have a fun time when I am coming. Lots of love Isabella xxxxxxxx

Isabella requested an envelope and packaged her gift and card.

A beautiful gift.

(Continued)

(Continued)

Isabella, what learning do I think is happening for you?

Isabella, you had a definite plan in mind today and knew exactly what you wanted to do. I was so impressed by your kind and caring attitude and the thoughtful way you went about making a gift for your grandma.

Isabella, you are such a kind and caring person. This was just one example; I often see you being a kind friend at kindergarten, making people feel special, either by including them in your play or helping them out when they are working through challenges.

Kindness is a disposition that we really value and celebrate at Roskill South Kindergarten. Just imagine, if there were more acts of kindness, what an impact that would make on our world! Isabella, I know you are going to make a difference and that you will continue to weave your kind ways wherever you go.

Arohanui Karen

(Arohanui means 'big love' in Māori)

Learning Story 4.2 An Act of Kindness

Strengthening the Portfolio as a Boundary Object: Introducing the Teachers and Adding DVDs

Karen R. is the Head Teacher at Isabella and Devya's kindergarten and her one-page biography, with photographs, is filed at the front of all the portfolios at the kindergarten; so are one-pagers from the other two teachers and the office staff. The teachers decided that, since they ask for information about the children and what they did at home, it was appropriate for the teachers to add information about themselves, and many centres do this now. Here is the text of Karen's Introduction:

> I grew up in Waiuku, a small country town south of Auckland. This is where I spent my childhood. My mum and dad still live there, while my brother Jason now lives in Perth. When I was 18 I left home and went to Teachers College in Christchurch. This was my first adventure living away from home. I always knew I wanted to travel … I travelled through many countries: the UK, Greek islands, Egypt and Turkey. … I started playing netball when I was 9! This photo is my grandma and me, I won a cup for playing netball when I was 14 years old. I must admit I am a Coronation Street fan; I have even been to the street in Manchester. Not once but twice! … I look forward to meeting you and your family and hearing your stories. This is my story. Stories are great – they help us make connections and form relationships. Let the story telling begin!

The children enjoy the photos of their teachers from the past, and the 'resumé' provides topics of conversation for teachers and new families to talk about

Writing in Hindi

13th September - Kim

This afternoon, I noticed Devya sitting at the table with his grandma.
As I watched, I saw Devya drawing symbols on his paper and heard his grandma talking to him and giving him directions.

Devya looked up and gave me a smile and then his grandma told me that he was writing in Hindi.
The communication between grandma and myself was quite limited but I was able to understand that Devya's grandma was a Hindi teacher in India and that she was teaching Devya to write in Hindi.

Devya proudly showed me his work and I was intrigued with the symbols he had written.

You are very clever, Devya, to be able to understand two languages. I certainly am not able to communicate in any other language and I'm sure you will pick up the English language very quickly.

A week later, after documenting your Hindi writing, your grandad came to kindergarten too. It was lovely to talk to him and I was able to get an insight into a little of your family life. Your grandparents are very proud of you and you are very special to them.
We love having them to visit at kindergarten and maybe your grandparents might like to come and see us again soon.
Does grandma like to cook? Maybe she might like to do some cooking at kindergarten with your friends. What do you think?

Learning Story 4.3   Writing in Hindi

together. DVDs are included in the children's portfolios as well and are watched at home. The opening quote in this chapter is from the mother of Kellen, who was attending Karen R.'s kindergarten. In the interview she adds: 'They love watching their DVDs all the time rather than watching Ben 10 or whatever: they would rather watch their own DVDs,' just as Julie had reported in Chapter 2 that, at another centre, a parent had watched her child's DVD eleven times. Karen adds:

We've found that DVDs just add another depth to our revisiting. A relatively cheap way of doing it these days is when you buy a big packet. So whenever the kids go on a trip or we have a group experience at kindergarten all the photos get put on a DVD and sometimes video footage. So they have this to take home, and some children choose to keep those DVDs in their portfolios and some choose to keep them at home. So they always have them to revisit, and we have found that this has really strengthened the links between home and centre and given the wider whānau [extended family] of that child a look into what is happening at kindergarten.

Strengthening the Portfolio as a Boundary Object: Including Home Languages

At Fa'amasani, a bilingual early childhood centre, the teachers write Learning Stories of events of interest, some in English and some in Samoan. Tunufa'i's family members at home in New Zealand and in Samoa monitor his development, with their particular interest in his memory of family events and (for the family back in Samoa) his facility with the Samoan language. In a conversation with Lusi (the teacher) about his portfolio, Tunufa'i talked about the photo of a recent trip to Samoa: he named the people, and Lusi commented on the order of the people that he named in 'what sounds like a family tree.' He also described the travel, using Lego bricks to make a model of the plane that they travelled in. One of the family members commented in Tunufa'i's portfolio: 'Tunufa'i's memory is quite good. He can tell stories of where he has been. A week since we were back from Samoa, while we were having dinner the other night, he started talking about the relatives and what they have done.' She added that the family in Samoa was impressed by Tunufa'i's Samoan language, even though he was born in New Zealand. An example from this centre, 'Peniamina builds a bridge', is included later in this chapter.

In a Learning Story in *Kei Tua o te Pae* (Carr, Lee and Jones, 2004, 3: 23) a parent contributes a story about her son, Jet, playing in the bath. She translates it into the home, Māori, language and adds a glossary of words in Māori that she would like the teachers to use. She is encouraging the teachers to use Māori in conversations with Jet at the centre and supporting the teachers' developing competence. The home language is also included in Learning Story 4.4; *Looking After Others!*

Strengthening the Portfolio as a Boundary Object: Adding Other Boundary Objects to the Stories

Just as home languages can straddle the boundaries of home and school inside Learning Stories and portfolios, so can objects that are deeply significant for the child. In Chapter 1 we quoted a comment about how when incoming knowledges

Looking after others!

18th February Teacher: Judy

Today we had some mums and grandmas cooking curry, rice and roti for the children. There was lamb and vegetable curry, vegetable curry, and tomato chutney – yum, yum! When all the food was ready, the children washed their hands then sat down on the mats outside while we dished up the curries in bowls.

Claire chose the lamb curry and rice and sat down on the step by the sandpit to eat it. You could see by looking at her just how much she was enjoying the food!

Mave sat down on the deck behind Claire, but didn't have any food. We tried encouraging him to have some, but he wasn't interested; however, as everyone was tucking in and enjoying the curries, Claire put her plate down, got up and walked over to the table chose a plate of curry and took it over and put it in front of Mave. She then returned to her own meal and continued eating! You are such a thoughtful, kind girl, Claire.

<u>What learning did I see happening here for Claire?</u>

Claire is showing an increasing ability to interact and care for other children. She was quick to understand and comprehend that while all the other children were enjoying their food, Mave was the only one without any.

Claire responded in a social, loving way, by ensuring Mave was looked after.

Well done, Claire!

关爱他人

二零一零年二月十八日
教师: 朱迪
今天，我们给孩子们做些家常的印度风味薄饼和咖喱饭，有咖喱羊肉蔬菜、咖喱蔬菜、番茄酱....味道美极! 食物准备妥当,孩子们洗了手坐在院子的席子上,我们给孩子们装盘。
克莱尔选了一盘咖喱羊肉饭便做在沙池旁台阶上吃了起来。
看到她吃饭的表情就知她有多喜欢吃这饭了!
马威坐在克莱尔身后的露台上，但什么也没吃。 我们劝他吃一点，但他不感兴趣。就在大家都在享用咖喱美食时，克莱尔放下盘子起身到桌前选了一盘咖喱饭端了过去放到马威面前.然后她又回到座位继续吃了起来!!你是这样一个细心善意的好姑娘,克莱尔。
克莱尔在这里学到了什么?
克莱尔表现出日益增长的与他人沟通和关爱他人的能力。她很快能注意到在大家享用美食时，马威是唯一没吃什么的人。
克莱尔以一种社交和爱心的方式确保马威受到关爱。做的好,克莱尔!

Learning Story 4.4   Looking After Others!

and dispositions from home and other places meet knowledges and learning dispositions at the early childhood centre, 'hybridisation of identity and multiple belongings are shaped' (Vandenbroeck, Roets and Snoeck, 2009: 211). A portfolio of events can reify and construct the journey of this process: turning it into an object, available for conversation, affirmation and re-cognition as the journey's direction shifts and turns. Emmanuel's family had arrived in New Zealand from a refugee camp in the Sudan. Emmanuel was born in New Zealand and came to the Family Centre when he was five months old. The Family Centre provided support for the refugee families and care and education for the children, often while their parents attended language classes. Robyn G., the teacher at the centre who wrote the story about Sela, the 'library girl' in Chapter 1, reflects on Emmanuel's first year at the centre:

> I noticed that Tabitha, Emmanuel's Mum, would give him a single animal from the basket and tell him something in Dinka (mother language) and he would appear to agree to stay in the centre. Before this we were at our wits end as he was continually highly stressed on arrival and we had no luck with getting near him, physically or with language, no strategies worked. ... Once I recognised Tabitha's strategy I was able to build on the animal interest with him, and other staff and children joined in.

The centre built up a *kete* (basket) of toy wild African animals that Emmanuel often took home with him, and a portfolio of Learning Stories about his interactions with these special animals. These 'boundary objects' assisted Emmanuel with 'multiple belongings'. The animals, and the Learning Stories about his play with them, enabled three-way conversations with Emmanuel's mother. The reflections from Robyn in Box 4.4 are accompanied by some of the photographs from the Learning Stories.

Box 4.4

Reflections from Robyn on Emmanuel's learning journey at the Family Centre

When Emmanuel is aged three

What we have learned is that through this intense interest, and our response, Emmanuel now allows all staff to approach him and also some other children, without becoming distressed. This has meant that we can talk about possibilities with him. The animals have become Emmanuel's and he has become the animal expert in our centre. ... In the past he has understood everything that I have talked to him about. I know this because his mother tells me. He tells his mother everything in his home language. For example I once suggested that he could be a doctor for the animals and his mother told me the next day that 'Emmanuel does not wish to be a doctor for the animals, he wishes to be known as the animals' friend.' He asked her to pass this message onto me. I enjoy these three-way conversations. That also reminds me of the funds of knowledge from home and the way they can be acknowledged and

included in the centre. He has taken some small steps away from the animals to explore some other interests but always returning to his beloved animals. He puts them to sleep and washes them, takes them out and one day he made a bus outside to give his giraffe a ride. He comes every day on the bus; sometimes he takes them home in his special little animal *kete*; he doesn't want to leave them at the centre. He calls the centre 'Roden's house': Roden is the Dinka name that he calls me. He has no concept of an early childhood centre and asks to come to my house. (All this from conversations with his mother.) … Emmanuel enjoys revisiting his folder (which contains his Learning Stories and photos) to check out his animals.

When Emmanuel is aged three-and-a-half

Emmanuel still has an animal interest today; however, the centre world is becoming much more enlarged. Going to the library for the very first time with us, it is a programme embedded in our centre and you can see him sitting there with a group of children. He's very interested in the stories. He sits with large groups and he listens avidly to many stories in English, because English is not his first language. He [now] talks to everyone and he shows us what he can do. … His English language has blossomed across this time. He can ask for help for anything and is putting sentences together and he knows the other children's

(Continued)

(Continued)

names and is making lots of friends. He's become very confident in his choices and he will carry his chair from morning teatime and place it beside whoever he wants to sit with.

When Emmanuel is aged four

We recently have had a wonderful Sudanese lady (Martha) come into the centre as a volunteer who speaks Emmanuel's language and provides great

 encouragement for him. It's actually Martha who encouraged him to paint. She tells him how things work. I recognised that this support has helped Emmanuel have a deeper understanding of the whole centre at last. ... Perhaps, with the toy animals, Emmanuel has been able to make some sense of some of his fears with other things in his and his family's life too.

Robyn adds a comment about agency that we interpret as also being a reference to the shaping of 'hybridisation of identity and multiple belongings': 'We are also thinking about agency: learning how to play the game. Knowing another game already.'

> [Emmanuel has found] a way into the socialising and friendship and playfulness that perhaps he can't experience by himself with just him and his animals. He does return to the animals frequently. The other day he was with us and in the afternoon he was tired but he spent all afternoon bathing the animals and towel drying them and did that for the whole afternoon. We were also thinking about agency: learning how to play the game. Knowing another game already.

At a nursery in Durham, three short stories are gathered together from 5, 12 and 18 May. Two of these stories are included in Learning Story 4.5. They describe Evie's developing sense of belonging in this new space and the title *Evie Comes Prepared* refers to her use of 'transition objects': Gee (a soft toy), 'blankie' (her blanket) and photos of the animals at home. Early in May she sorts out what can go into her bag and what can be held. In a final comment, on 18 May, the teacher, Debby, writes:

Evie comes prepared

It was great meeting you, Evie, when you came to see us with Mummy and Daddy. I knew you were going to be a character and you haven't disappointed!

Gee and blankie!

May 5th

You came fully prepared for adventure as you arrived at nursery, with dummy, blankie and Gee. You bravely kissed goodbye to Daddy and gave him a big hug. You shed a few tears as he left and we found out Daddy's a softy at heart when he returned for one last cuddle before saying he'd be back...and he did come back, Evie!

Mummy had told us you love being with older children but, as everything is new, you are happy exploring your new environment and getting to know where everything is, especially new jungle friends for Gee. You even had a little tea party for him!

May 12th

Today you brought in photos of Murphy and your cats, Chilly and Tilly. ☺ How cool is that?! You were more than happy to show your new friends but didn't want to put the photos on the wall...of course you didn't, they are your pets. So you took them around with you, but you were finding it a little tricky to carry everything by now! You were keen to help Toby complete the Snow White jigsaw, but struggled with what to put down! Then I remembered your bag: "Let's put everything in your bag and then you can carry it and finish the jigsaw." 'Evie the organiser' set to work sorting out what could go in the bag and what needed to be held. You felt comfortable putting Murphy and blankie in the bag – you've already begun leaving it on your bed after nap time and your dummy only comes out then too – so Gee and the cats stayed close and shortly after, Snow White was complete.

Success all round!

Learning Story 4.5   Evie Comes Prepared

What next for Evie: Evie is embracing her time at nursery and there are many potential new friends …. I think she is currently sussing them all out!! She's working out
how to manage play and Gee and I think she'll come to her own happy conclusion
as to where and when he fits in.

Making Connections with the Wider Community Outside the Early Childhood Centre or Classroom

Learning Stories that make connections with the wider community can be
initiated by the learners, the teachers or the families. A Learning Story from
Tunufa'i's centre, in Peniamina's portfolio, reflects his connection between
the key shapes (triangles) in a bridge that he has seen and the opportunities
to represent these with resources at the centre (coloured popsicle sticks). The
writer of this story comments on the conversation with Peniamina (see
Learning Story 4.6 *Peniamina's Bridge: O le auala laupapa a Peniamina*), especially on his competence in Samoan and his memory of the bridge.

In a paper entitled 'Growing raukura', Brenda Soutar and the Mana Tamariki
whānau (2010) write that the Mana Tamariki kōhanga Reo Centre of Innovation
research project has been built on:

> the notion of te tamaiti hei raukura – the child as a high achiever who exemplifies
> the hopes and aspirations of their people. … Our research question asked 'How can we
> strengthen the reciprocal relationships between te reo, children as raukura, whānau
> and Paki Ako?' … Paki Ako is a term that explains the method we use to document
> and assess learning in our kōhanga reo. Mana Tamariki developed Paki Ako as our
> adaptation of Learning Stories. (p. 38)

Three examples of paki ako are included in this book: one in this chapter, and
two that were written during the development of a *māra tapu*, a sacred garden,
initiated during the research project under the wise guidance and counsel of
a *kaumatua* (elder), Professor Te Wharehuia Milroy. The story 'Te Kohikohi
Pūtea' begins with a saying or proverb, a *whakatauki*: 'With your basket and
my basket, the people will be provided for.' In September 2010 and again in
February 2011, a major city in the South Island of New Zealand, Christchurch,
suffered great damage and hardship and considerable loss of life in major
earthquakes. The kōhanga family – teacher, children and whānau – decided
to go into the city centre in their home town in the North Island 'as a way of
sending our aroha [sympathy, love] to the many families affected in
Christchurch'. The group paki ako (see Learning Story 4.7, *Te Kohikohi Pūtea*)
describes the traditional way in which this was done, performing *haka* (a fierce
ceremonial dance) and *waiata* (chant, song). The story of the assessment journey in this kōhanga reo, with some more examples, is told in the publication
Te Whatu Pōkeka (Ministry of Education, 2009a: 80) where they write that:

O le auala laupapa a Peniamina
23rd June Teacher: Lusila

Ao fai fauga fale a Peniamina ma Ielemia e faaaoga fasilaau o aisa poloka. Fai mai Ielemia o lona fale la e fai. Sa fai mai Peniamina o lau auala laupapa lea o loo fai. O le vaa lea o loo fealuai I lalo o le auala laupapa. Matua maualuga le fausia ina o lau auala laupapa. "O le auala lea sa vaai ai au." I fea o lau fesili lea. "I le pasi." Ina ua oo mai le matou pasi I luga o le auala laupapa i North Shore o Peniamina sa ia faailoa I tamaiti o lea ua matou I luga ole bridge (auala laupapa). I lalo o le auala laupapa o loo feoai ai vaa i luga o le sami. Sa faanoanoa Peniamina ina ua faaleaga e Uelese lana auala laupapa. Sa ou fai ia Uelese, Uelese faamolemole aua le faaleagaina le auala laupapa a Peniamina sa tigaina e fai. Na o le luelue mai o lona ulu ma ia toe tago toe tuu faalelei le fasilaau sa ia faaleagaina. Ua malie le loto o Peniamina ona faaauau lea o le fausiaina o lana auala laupapa.

Iloiloga

Ao fai le fale a Peniamina sa ia toe manatuina i le fauina o lona fale le auala laupapa sa ia vaai i ai i le aso na alu ai le matou tafaoga i le pasi. Na amata mai I le fauina o le fale, ae na toe suia i le auala laupapa ina ua uma ona fau le fale, ua le fale ae ua auala laupapa. Ao fausiaina lana auala laupapa e tele mea sa ia aoaoina mai I le galuega faatino sa ia faia. O lanu o fasilaau sa ia faaaogaina, o siepi, faapea ai ma le faatauaina o le gagana Samoa o loo faaaogaina i talatalanoaga. E le gata i lea ae o le mataala ma le faaaogaina o lona mafaufau e toe manatuaina ai le auala laupapa sa vaai iai i le aso na alu ai tafaoga a le aoga, e ala lea i le fausiaina o le auala laupapa e foliga i le auala laupapa sa ia vaai iai.

Manatu o matua

O le auala laupapa a Peniamina: Peniamina's Bridge
23rd June

Peniamina and Ieremia were building, using the coloured iceblock sticks. Ieremia was building his house, while Peniamina said he was building a bridge. "This is a boat going under the bridge," said Peniamina.
"What a very high bridge." said the teacher.
"I have seen this bridge" he said.
"Where did you see it?" asked the teacher.
Peni replied, "On the bus. As we came over the bridge in North Shore. Under the bridge I saw boats on the sea."
Uelese tried to help, but Peniamina was not happy. He continued with his bridge making.

Analysis:
While the building was taking place, Peniamina remembered how it looked like the bridge when they went travelling on a bus. The building started off as a house and then transformed into a bridge, like the one to North Shore. There was a lot more talking happening about the shapes he had made, the colours of the sticks, the rich use of the Samoan language, and the sharp memory of how the bridge looked, and where he had seen it.

Learning Story 4.6   Peniamina's Bridge: *O le aula laupapa a Peniamina*

We have learned that we cannot 'master' assessment. As with a Māori world view, the process is continually emerging and our understanding is constantly evolving. The realisation that each learning story fulfils numerous purposes astounds us. One story becomes an assessment of learning and teaching for all, a language resource, a documentation of history, a planning tool, a report, a piece of evidence for external agencies – and the list goes on.

Devya's portfolio at Karen R.'s kindergarten includes a Learning Story written on his first day. Entitled 'Welcome to Kindergarten', it includes photographs of him playing in the sandpit, and a note to him, explaining that: 'This is your special portfolio where we will put stories about your adventures and learning at kindergarten. Your family can write stories to put in your folder too.' An early story of his writing in Hindi with his grandmother at the kindergarten has been included earlier in this chapter. The commentary added that a week later, after documenting this Hindi writing, the grandfather also came to kindergarten. Kim, one of the teachers, added that: 'I was able to get an insight into a little of your family life.' The teachers documented many examples of Devya at work, and they came to realise the cultural significance of many of his interests and explorations; Devya often talked to the teachers about temple visits in India. He found a picture of a peacock and struggled to draw it, and later, when he decided that he would like to make a mosaic tile, the teacher recalled his passion for peacocks. Devya completed a mosaic tile of a peacock and the process was recorded in photographs and text. His father explained to the teachers that his passion for peacocks came from his huge interest in Krishna (who always appears with a peacock feather on the top of his head). A shorter story entitled *Temple Design* (Learning Story 4.8) is included here, in which Karen and Devya consult a website for pictures of temples, and then Devya builds a temple with blocks.

Concluding Comments

This chapter has explored the notion that the construction of learner identities includes negotiated experiences across communities. Etienne Wenger has maintained that: 'We define who we are by the ways we reconcile our various forms of membership into one identity' (1998: 149). Elsewhere we have acknowledged that learner selves are multifaceted (Carr, Smith, Duncan, Jones, Lee and Marshall, 2010: 198), and some thoughts about these reconciliations as 'balances' will appear in Chapter 7. The idea in Wenger's *Communities of practice* (1998) that summarises much of the discussion in this chapter, however, is when he argues that the ability to apply learning from one place and one situation to another is not a matter of abstracting the content, an informational question, 'it is more

Te Kohikohi Pūtea
"Nāku te rourou, nāu te rourou, ka ora ai te iwi"

I puea ake te whakaaro ākuni pea he tū i te taone waiata ai tā tātou mahi hei kawe i te aroha o Mana Tamariki ki ngā whānau ki Ōtautahi e pani ana, me kore e tūpono he paku maramara hei āpiti atu ki te rourou a te motu e whakaritea nei.

Nō te ata o te tuatoru o Poutū-te-rangi, i kotahi atu tātou ki te pokapū o te taone ki te haka, ki te waiata. Te ātaahua, te wera hoki o te rā. Nō tātou tonu te whiwhi! Tīmata ana ngā mahi haka ka toia mai e koutou te minenga. Nā te rōreka o ō koutou reo pea te take? Nā te pūkanakana mai o ō koutou mata, nā te ātaahua o te piu o ō koutou tinana pea?

I kawea ake e tēnā, e tēnā te mānuka. Tū ana ko ihi, tū ana ko wehi! Whakamīharo ana te iwi i ā koutou nā mahi. Ko ō koutou mātua hoki ērā i puta ki te tautoko i te kaupapa o te rā.

Nāu, Moera, te rourou i pupuri. I kite au i tō urupū ki tāu nā mahi me te nui o tō hari. Tēnā rā koe! Nā kōrua, Te Rahikoi kōrua ko Rakei Te Kura, te pānui i pupuri e mārama pai ai te iwi he aha rā ia te take o tā tātou tūnga i te taone waiata ai.

Ka wani kē kōrua me tā kōrua mahi tahi.

Otirā, i ū koutou katoa, tamariki mā! Whakahī ana a roto i te rangatira o tā koutou tū, nā reira e taea ai te kī kua ea, kua tutuki pai te wāhi ki te kohikohi pūtea.

E $719 te huinga pūtea i kohia e Mana Tamariki i te 45 mēneti noa iho! Ka mau kē te wehi!

Fundraising
"With your food basket and my food basket, the people will be provided for."

We decided to go into the city centre and sing, as a way of sending our aroha to the many families affected in Christchurch. We hoped our efforts busking would raise some funds that could then be added to the nationwide collection.

On 3.3.11, we went to the mall to perform haka and waiata. It was a beautiful day and the sun was warm. How fortunate we were! As soon as you began your performance, you pulled a crowd. Maybe it was your beautiful singing voices? Maybe it was the way your faces performed the pūkana, or the beautiful way in which your bodies swayed?

Moera, you held the bucket for the community to contribute. I saw how responsible you were about this task and how happy you were. Thank you! Te Rahikoi, you and Rakei Te Kura held the poster that explained to bystanders why we were performing. You did an awesome job working together. I was so proud of the way in which you all stood, so dignified, and that's why it is able to be said that you did it! You achieved the goal. $719 was raised. That was awesome! Each one of you took up the challenge. There was a feeling of exhilaration and excitement!

Learning Story 4.7   Te Kohikohi Pūtea

fundamentally a question of identity, because identity is the vehicle that carries our experiences from context to context' (p. 268). And we suggest that documenting and discussing the interconnections between making meaning in a range of complex environments and contexts contributes to this multifaceted identity. Learning Stories have a powerful role to play for learners by documenting this reconciliation. The children here were recontextualising their understandings across communities. Emma, a

Temple Design

20th November
Karen

Today Devya requested to look at the gods, particularly Krishna: "In your computer, and we can print a picture," he explained. While we were re-visiting the website, I remembered our new blocks that had recently been delivered. The blocks are gorgeous, lovely wood in amazing and different shapes, similar to those shapes used for temples and special buildings around the world. I suggested to Devya that we could open the box and have a look at our new blocks. You can imagine Devya's delight when he discovered the beautiful shapes, as he straight away began to make connections with his temple.

Devya began designing and constructing his temple, playing around with different ideas and experimenting with the different shapes. Using the picture we had printed earlier, Devya now began to draw his ideas and thoughts. After a little while, Devya placed the picture behind his temple and said, "The gods will not fit." He then tried the picture from the printer but they still would not fit.

I could see his dilemma. Devya went on to explain that the gods live inside the temple and that they would not fit in the temple that he had built.

I remembered there were some smaller photos on the website, so we went back to the computer and I showed Devya the smaller view.

Devya thought this size could work, so we printed out a page. Devya returned to his temple where he cut out the picture. Just the perfect size!

What learning do I think is happening for Devya?

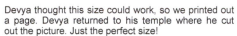

Devya continues to direct his own learning and he knows where to access the information he needs to support his further learning. Devya likes to revisit his interest through the Mandir website and he knows this is where he can source pictures of the gods.

Devya also continues to develop his own working theories about his interest in the Hindu gods, and he shares his ideas with his friends and teachers. Devya certainly has an interest in exploring and researching and he has a real thirst for knowledge. His spatial awareness is developing, he explores how two- and three-dimensional objects can fit together and the size required to get just the right look he is looking for.

I will share the Mandir DVD with Devya. This may provide new knowledge and inspiration.

Learning Story 4.8   Temple Design

classroom teacher in the *Transition to School* project, made the following comment about the role of Learning Stories in this process.

> (This boy) didn't speak a word for probably a week or so and then he brought his kindy book [*portfolio of Learning Stories*] in and it was like a new child emerged and it was like this is me and this is who I am and even though I don't necessarily have the language to tell you, I can show you with pictures. And I would turn around at all times of the day and hear little murmurings and laughing and there would be pockets of children sitting around this little boy with his kindy book. (Emma, New Entrant school teacher)

The portfolio can thus be a particularly powerful recontextualising tool, and in this chapter the Learning Stories and other border-crossing objects and processes worked together to blur the boundaries and assist in the development of multifaceted identities and multiple belongings: rich and complex possible selves who are disposed to improvise, innovate and critique. Table 4.1 sets out some thoughts about this recontextualisation in practice for some of the children. The boundary-crossing objects that have done some of the recontextualising work (in addition to the Learning Stories and portfolios) are italicised: the photographs, a letter attached to a necklace, home languages, funds of knowledge from home, toy animals that travelled, Gee (a soft toy), haka and waiata. Table 4.1 also attempts to illustrate the notion of 'split screen' analysis by separating out the stores of subject knowledge and the stores of disposition that were being called on (and strengthened) in eight examples.

Table 4.1 Examples of a split-screen analysis, boundary crossing and recontextualising objects and processes

Stores of subject knowledge	Stores of disposition	The boundary-crossing object or process in addition to the portfolio: the recontextualising
Paige. Recalling an event in sequence: language and literacy	*Re-storying for others who were not there*	*Photographs,* being expected to explain
Isabella. Using beads as a resource: technology, design, art	*Being kind,* making a present for a grandmother in hospital	Adding a *letter* to the boundary object (the *necklace*) to label its destination across a number of borders
Devya. Writing in Hindi: literacy Expertise on Indian gods and temples: religious studies and cultural practices	*Being sensitive to occasion,* speaking and writing in the home language, Hindi, at the kindergarten, a mostly English-speaking environment, with the grandmother present who does not speak English. *Being multimodal:* using a website and blocks to represent this expertise	Shifting from one *language* to another, 'reading' the culture at this kindergarten and knowing that this was legitimate and valued Using *photographs* as a guide, shifting from drawing to building on the same topic
Emmanuel. Knowing about a new country, a new place: social and cultural studies	*Belonging in a new place,* socialising and playfulness	Taking *funds of knowledge from home* into the centre: knowledge and stories about wild animals, the *toy animals* themselves
Evie. Playing in the family corner: drama	*Finding a place for transition objects* across the boundary from their normal site	Working out how to manage play and *Gee* at the same time
Peniamina. Making patterns with the coloured iceblock sticks: mathematics	*Remembering* a bridge seen from the bus and *representing* it using the sticks	Being expected to explain, tell a story, requiring the 'rich use of the *Samoan language*'
Children at the kōhanga reo. Performing a group haka and waiata: cultural practices	*Taking responsibility* to employ the haka and waiata to support a city after an earthquake	Remaining 'dignified', as appropriate for *the haka and waiata,* in an unusual situation
Claire. Eating curry: food technology, nutrition	Deferring her own task, *looking after* another	The *home language* travels with her

Notes

1 The indicators for 'vulnerable' for this purpose included a high level of unemployment, a high degree of transience, a high proportion of single parent families and a high proportion of the population under the age of 25.
2 The notion of 'reification' is a useful one for discussions about documenting learning and achievement. The word has been used in at least two ways in the

education literature. Anna Sfard (2008) writes that it is a process of turning processes into nouns, and in the *Learning in the making* book we turned the nouns of three dispositions – reciprocity, resilience and imagination – back into verbs so that we could recognise the actions that they represent. Relevant to this book's topic, see also an interesting paper by Anna Sfard and Anna Prusak from 2005 on 'Telling identities: In search of an analytical tool for investigating learning as a cultural activity', in which they introduce their position on p. 15: 'Lengthy deliberations led us to the decision to *equate identities with stories about persons*. No, no mistake here: We did not say that identities were *finding their expression in stories* – we said that they were stories. On the other hand, Wenger (1998) uses the concept of 'reification' to refer to the process of giving form to our experience by realising it, turning it into a concrete material object, as in documentation. 'In so doing we create points of focus around which the negotiation of meaning becomes organised'(p. 58). Wenger notes (p. 65) that: 'The complementarity of participation and reification yields an obvious but profound principle for endeavours that rely on some degree of continuity of meaning', and he writes about the need for a balancing of these. If participation prevails (if most of what matters is left unreified), then there might not be enough material to anchor the learning journey and to uncover the assumptions. If reification prevails (if everything is reified), then there may be little opportunitiy for shared experience and interactive negotiation.

3 In Book 5 (*Assessment and learning: Community*) of *Kei Tua o te Pae* there are seven exemplars of Learning Stories that link the early childhood centre to home and community; Book 3 includes eight 'bicultural' stories.

5

Recognising and Re-cognising Learning Continuities

Box 5.1

How does the questioning begin? We wonder about this. What is it that sets our babies on this curious path of discovery and how can we be supportive resources? For some time now we've been thinking of babies in the same way as our toddlers and young children – as researchers – learners who make discoveries about the world through investigation. So with this view of the infant researcher in my head, over several months now I've been watching Ruby very closely and I think she gives us a clue. As with all our very young babies we give them a safe interesting place to stretch and move as they choose at the end of our infant [baby] room. There are a range of textures to explore and, at this very beginning, it provides a cosy place for family and child to get to know their new setting. Something happens here. As I watched Ruby's sense of belonging deepening – establishing that this was an interesting, OK place to be – she started to explore. (Lorraine, an introductory paragraph in a Learning Story about Ruby)

Lorraine is writing about continuity over time, wondering about how an early childhood centre sets and sustains a path of exploration. She is arguing that giving babies a safe interesting place to stretch and move as they choose is a good starting place and that as Ruby's sense of belonging deepened, she started to explore. Many later Learning Stories in Ruby's portfolio (see Learning Story 5.1, *Ruby's Exploration*) document that exploration over her almost five years at her early childhood centre.

Continuity over time can refer to the past in the longest sense, and it can refer to the future in the longest sense too: as a possible self, an aspirational identity. Jay Lemke (2000: 273) begins a paper on 'Across the scales of time' with two questions: How do *moments* add up to *lives*? and How do our shared

Ruby's Exploration

Ruby is setting off on her exploration. She had been planning this exploration for some time.

Now she sets her goals well beyond the confines of the infant spaces, and stretches herself in very interesting environments.

Ruby continues to challenge herself in a variety of contexts, looking forward to the challenge of attempting the climbing wall. In the first climbing wall story she says, "I climbed to the top. It was scary because the wind was blowing. I could see a long way up there. I had to work hard to climb."

In the story in Ruby's folder about Ruby rock climbing, Ruby's mother writes, "Her bravery even extended to her little brother Jack – who followed her up the biggest rocks – and even to her mum, who doesn't like heights much. Who knows where this rock climbing confidence will take her – and the rest of the family!"

Learning Story 5.1   Ruby's Exploration

moments together add up to *social life* as such? He develops a table of the scales of time: from an exchange of seconds to minutes, to an episode of a few minutes to an hour, to a 'lesson', to a lifespan of educational development. He notes that longer-term processes and shorter-term events can be linked by 'boundary objects' (p. 281), which are typically records that link times, places and events both as a material object and as a *sign* or *text*. In another paper entitled 'The long and the short of it' (2001: 21), Lemke develops this idea by saying that one type of 'tracer', tracing the development over time, that might be of particular value is, 'A material object that carries significant information across time and space and that serves, through local interpretation, to create coherence between distal events.' He introduces the notion of 'significant chains of episodes' that share common features,[1] and then asks: 'How are we to know which features matter?'. He says that we have to look one more level up, and ask 'For what still longer term processes do these chains matter?'

Writing in the same journal issue, Sasha Barab, Kenneth Hay and Lisa Yamagata-Lynch (2001) emphasise a 'learning in the middle' frame of reference as outlined in Chapter 1 of this book: learning continuities as trajectories of individual–environment interactions. They comment:

Our focus is primarily on tracing the events through which an individual or a number of individuals come to engage in a specific practice, understand a particular concept, evolve their use of a resource, or construct a particular artifact. The important methodological challenge is to portray the practice or understanding as a contextualized trajectory of individual–environment interactions and not as abstract concepts residing in the individual's head. This requires that researchers are able to describe not only the actor's actions but also the environmental conditions that were the focus and that constrained these actions. (p. 71)

This chapter illustrates two ways in which Learning Stories contribute to the recognising and re-cognising of continuities: as links in significant chains of learning episodes, and as opportunities to construct continuities and to make them visible.

Learning Stories as Links in Significant Chains of Learning Episodes

Learning Stories can act as 'material objects that carry significant information across time and space', create coherence between events and refer to longer term processes to construct significant chains of learning episodes. The *Te Kohikohi Pūtea* (fundraising for the earthquake fund) example in the previous chapter lasted half a day, and the longer term process that made it significant was expressed in the whakatauki – belonging to a caring cultural community where each person's contribution is valued. These longer term processes can refer to a cultural continuity that goes far back into time:

The child was, and still is, the incarnation of the ancestors: te kanohi ora, 'the living face'. The child was, and still is, the living link with yesterday and the bridge to tomorrow: te taura here tangata, 'the binding rope that ties people together over time'. The child is the kāwai tangata, the genealogical link, that strengthens whanaungatanga, 'family relationships' of that time and place. (Reedy, 2003: 58)

This notion of continuity is reflected in te māra tapu, the sacred garden project at Te kōhanga Reo o Mana Tamariki. This project is described by Brenda Soutar (2010) who includes the text of a karakia (a prayer-chant) gifted to Mana Tamariki by the kaumatua Te Wharehuia Milroy. She explains how the karakia is used:

It is used to erect row markers in the garden and for planting. It is one example of how the knowledge held by the whānau of Mana Tamariki was deepened through our Centre of Innovation project. This knowledge will in time be imparted to the children, and intergenerational transmission of a Māori way of knowing and being will be in process. (p. 35)

During the development of the garden, kaiako (teachers) wrote paki ako (their adaptation of Learning Stories) to reflect the knowing-in-the-making embedded in the māra project. Sometimes these stories were written with a lens that zoomed out to emphasise the nature of a māra tapu and 'the intergenerational transmission of a Māori way of knowing and being'. Box 5.2 includes an excerpt (translated into English here) from one of the early stories.

Box 5.2

O Rongo

An excerpt from a paki ako, written by Amy. Translation into English from the Māori. [Two toddlers take their 'babies' for a stroll through the garden. They greet Papa Waaka who is working in the garden and he shows them around. He pulls some carrots for them, washes them, and they say a karakia kai (karakia or prayer associated with food) before they sit in the garden to eat them.]

… I noticed Rangitahuri and Apirana walking around the garden observing the luscious vegetables in the garden. They touched the tomatoes, greeting them with respect "Hello tomatoes". Again Rangitahuri speaks of her knowledge of the garden rules. "Be careful Apirana, don't grab the tomatoes, leave them to grow". Apirana demonstrates his understanding and nods his head: "Yes, they are still growing. They are small". … Today Apirana and Rangitahuri demonstrated their knowledge of the customary practices in the garden, … [They] demonstrated their knowledge specific to karakia kai. I observed their learning and how they can transfer these customs to other contexts, even though there was only a small portion of food. Apirana and Rangitahuri are on the right path in their learning abilities for their age group.

One year later, Rea wrote a group story about the children in the garden, providing another story that will be read back to the children at the centre and at home, with three lenses in mind: as part of their language development strategy; to document the development of the māra tapu; and to trace the children's appropriation of some of the cultural practices associated with it (see Learning Story 5.2 *Anuhe Ringa Rehe!*). The kaiako (teachers) also refer to Te Whāriki as well as a guiding document for Maōri schools, Te Aho Matua,

Anuhe ringa rehe!
Ki ro pārekereke, whitikina e te rā
Mākuku i te ua, te waiora e i!

Nō mua tonu i tā tātou putanga atu ki waho, ka whakamārama atu au ki a koutou ko tā tātou i te rangi nei he huhuti kānga hei kai mā te whānau. "Kua pakeke ngā kānga ināianei?" te ui a Te Koomuri Aroha. "Ae, kua pakari. Kua pakari i tā koutou, otirā, i tā tātou maimoa, i tā tātou tauwhiro pai i te māra kai," tāku i whakahoki atu.

"Tēnā rā koe e te māra!" tā koutou tamariki mā i tā tātou putanga atu ki waho, me taku mihi ki te rangatira o ō koutou nā whakaaro Māori, ki tā koutou whai whakaaro ki te tuku mihi atu ki te māra, ki ngā hua, otirā, ki a Rongo, ki a Haumia.

I kite atu tātou i a Pou Waaka i tawhiti, i te māra kai kē a ia e tatari mai ana ki a tātou.

Ahakoa tāku ki a koutou kia piri mai ki a au, auare ake! Ka tukuna e koutou te taura ka oma, korakora ana te haere, wehe ana i te rekareka! "Kia ora Pāpā Waaka", "Tēnā koe Pāpā Waaka", "Kia ora Pāpā Waaka" tāu Rakei Te Kura, te kākā o te rōpū Anuhe! Ka nui rā tō aroha ki a Pou Waaka, neha? Otirā, i roto i ngā wiki tata nei kua kite atu au ko koutou katoa tamariki mā e aroha nui ana ki a ia! Ka mau kē te wehi!

Nō te taenga atu ki te māra kai, hohoro ana tā koutou tautoko i a Pou Waaka ki te huhuti kānga, ka pīhoretia e koutou ngā pakere ka makaia atu ki te papa. Katahi te hunga ringa raupā ko koutou e kare mā!

I reira au e ata mātakitaki atu ana i a koutou, ā, i kite au arā anō ētahi i whakamātau i te kānga, i ngata. "Mmmmmm te reka hoki," tāku i rongo ai me taku whakamīharo ka tika! Hī ana ngā pewa, menemene mai ana ngā mata i te reka o te wai kānga, warawara ana te hiakai i te wainene! Ka puku kata a roto i taku ohorere i kainga e koutou e mata tonu ana, mā te aha i tēnā e hoa mā!

Ka mihi ra au ki a koutou, e te rōpū Anuhe, anuhe ringa rehe! Me ā koutou mahi rangatira i te rangi nei! Mutu ana ngā mahi i te māra, heke ana a mōtuhi, mākuku ana a rae i te pukumahi, nanea ana a tia, puta ana a pito! "E noho rā e te māra!" tā koutou. Ka hoki atu tātou ki te whare o te kōhanga reo.

Nā Rea Te 16 o ngā rā o Poutū te rangi

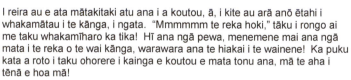

(Continued)

(Continued)

Anuhe expert hands!
In the garden, bathed by the sun's rays,
moistened by the rain, well-being and good health!

Before we ventured outside, I explained to you all that today we were going to pick the corn for the whole whānau to eat. "Has the corn grown up?" Te Koomuri Aroha asked. "Yes, it's ready. It's ready because of your, actually all of our, collective caring and nurturing of the garden," I replied.

"Hello garden!" all of you children called on arrival outside, and I praise you all for how well you think with Māori thoughts, that you know we should talk to the garden, to the vegetables and to the gods of this domain Rongo and Haumia.

We saw Pou Waaka in the distance, waiting for you all in the garden.

Even though I asked you all to stay close to me, it was to no avail! You dropped the rope and ran, speeding along, so happy! "Kia ora Pāpā Waaka", "Tēnā koe Pāpā Waaka", "Kia ora Pāpā Waaka" you called, Rakei Te Kura, the parrot of the Anuhe group! You love Pou Waaka to bits, don't you? Well, in the last few weeks I have seen a lot of love from all of you for him! That's awesome!

When we arrived in the garden, you were quick to help Pou Waaka pick the corn, stripping away the husks and discarding them on the ground. You were so ready to get your hands dirty!

I was there watching you all and I saw some of you try the corn and you liked it. "Mmmmmm it's really sweet," I heard you say and I was quite amazed! With eyebrows raised, you all had big smiles tasting the sweetness of the corn juice, whetting your appetites. It was so delicious! I laughed to myself because I was surprised you ate the corn uncooked – you can't ask for much more than that!

I want to acknowledge you all, the Anuhe group, Anuhe expert hands! What an excellent job you did today! By the time we had finished in the garden we were sweating, our brows were glistening from our hard work and our stomachs were full. "Bye bye garden!" you all said. And we went back inside the kōhanga reo.

By Rea 16th March

Learning Story 5.2 Anuhe Ringa Rehe!

and listen to the advice of their elders to ensure the essence of the practices remain spiritually, culturally, linguistically, pedagogically and administratively Māori (Soutar, 2010: 37).

As Jay Lemke has said: 'it becomes essential to consider *classroom* dynamics both in relation to *individual* activities, identities and trajectories and in relation to *broader school and community* contexts' (2001: 18) (our emphasis). Writing about maths classroom-based research he asks:

> Why do we observe students on the time scale of the lesson, inside the maths classroom, and not follow them out the door, down the hall, to another classroom, lunchroom, street corner, work, or home? … We can see the short-term development of a meaningful practice, but not the longer development of a meaning-making disposition, an attitudinal stance, a habitus (Bourdieu, 1990). (Lemke, 2001: 20)

The teachers in this book often had their eye on the longer development of meaning-making dispositions. Nikki and Susie (Chapter 2) referred to the children's criteria for the school curriculum key competency 'participation' to trace one of the chains of significance (trying something new in different places) in Diana's portfolio. In the *Cross Country* Learning Story (Chapter 3) Michael was using the five key competencies from the school curriculum as a guide to author his own Learning Story. These five competencies have been translated into four learner identities at his school: communicator, resilient learner, thinker and caring citizen. The Learning Story format includes the local school indicators for each of these and Michael has highlighted 'resilient learner' and 'persevere with tasks' and included these words in his story. Four values are also included on the assessment format: respect, curiosity, personal best and honesty, and Michael has referenced one of these as he tells his story. At two centres, courage as a value is foregrounded in some of their stories, as it was for Diana in Chapter 2. One of these is a New Zealand kindergarten (see Learning Story 5.3, *A Challenge at Kindergarten*) and the second is an early childhood centre in Berlin (see Learning Story 5.4, *Christina's Learning Experience*).

Zeb's teachers (Chapter 3) were implicitly referring to one of the outcomes 'working theories about the living world and how to care for it' in Te Whāriki to trace Zeb's growing interest in, expert knowledge of, and theorising about, fish. In Chapter 4, the tracing of Evie's early days at the nursery, as she was 'working out how to manage play and Gee' (Learning Story 4.5, *Evie Comes Prepared*) implicity refers to a valued longer term process: belonging and exploration.

In a Learning Story entitled *Kieran the Book Maker* from a classroom in Berkshire, England, the teacher, Debbie, refers to two aspects of a learning environment from the Early Years Foundation stage ('Young children require space, indoors and outdoors, where they can be active or quiet, and where they can think, dream and watch others' and 'Children learn from first-hand experiences') to note the facilitating environment for longer development of which this story is part: the development of language and vocabulary (see Learning Story 5.5, *Kieran the Book Maker*).

In a New Zealand early childhood centre, teachers developed three qualities of a 'Super Learner Hero'.[2] Being a Super Learner is described by a certain action, and denoted in the Learning Story by an icon in the corner of the Learning Story. The three actions are: focusing (a yellow cape), practising (a blue cape), and thinking (a green cape). Stories of these actions are shared with the group, when the learner wears the cape (see one of the three posters that are included in the children's portfolios, in Learning

A challenge at Kindergarten

Getting from one tree to the other!

21st July   By Jo

This afternoon, there was a huge amount of interest around the two trees growing at Kindergarten. Aidan approached Joceline and explained that a rope could be used to get from one side to the other. What an awesome idea! And so it was that a 'rope bridge' was built between both trees. It wasn't long before a larger group of children formed to take on the challenge of crossing the great divide. Joceline was on hand to provide encouragement as, one by one, the great crossing was made.

What learning is happening here?

Georgia, you showed great courage and confidence today. I like the way that you took your time to observe others climbing from one tree to the other. And then you were off, you decided it was your time and you were ready to give it a go. With lots of encouragement, you carefully negotiated your way from one tree to the other.

Georgia, your determination and perseverance have been a driving force in your ability to master the 'rope bridge'. You were provided with a challenge and, as seen in your DVD, your sense of accomplishment was huge. Ka mau te wehi - you rock!

Courage=hautoa
Confidence=maia!
Perseverance=u-tonu-tanga
Determination-hiringa

Learning Story 5.3   A Challenge at Kindergarten

Christina's learning experience

8th August, Hatun

Today, when we all were at the playground, Christina was very interested in the slide. She first observed the other children for a long time, as they climbed up the ladder and then happily slid down. But she did not yet fully trust herself to approach the seemingly large object. I watched Christina and could see that she was both fascinated and overwhelmed by the size of the slide; however, after a few minutes, she decided to take a step towards the mysterious slide. At first, she climbed up the ladder timidly and unsteadily. Once she reached the top, I could sense her insecurity, as she realised that, no matter what, she now had to slide down. She mustered all her courage, sat on the slide and slid down. As she reached the ground, she was relieved but also full of joy at having overcome her initial scepticism and having had so much fun. After this achievement, the slide was her favourite place of the day. Each time she slid down, she was just as excited as she had been the first time.

Christina learned to overcome her fears. She had a sense of achievement and had a great time!

Lerngeschichte von Christina

8. August, Hatun

Als wir alle zusammen auf den Spielplatz gegangen sind, war Christina sehr an der Rutsche interessiert. Zunächst beobachtete sie die anderen Kinder aufmerksam und sah ihnen eine Zeit lang zu, wie diese die Leiter hinaufkletterten und anschließend freudig hinunterrutschten. Doch sie selbst wagte sich noch nicht so recht an das groß erscheinende Ding heran. Ich sah Christina zu, wie sie einerseits fasziniert und andererseits überwältigt von der Größe der Rutsche war. Nach einigen Minuten fasste sie den Entschluss doch eine Schritt auf die geheimnisvolle Rutsche zuzugehen. Anfangs stieg sie ängstlich und wackelig die Leiter hinauf. Als sie oben ankam konnte ich ihre Unsicherheit sehen, da sie jetzt, egal was auch passierte wieder hinunter muss. Sie packte allen ihren Mut zusammen, setzte sich auf die Rutsche und rutschte hinunter. Unten angekommen war sie erleichtert und zugleich voller Freude ihre anfängliche Skepsis überwunden zu haben und noch soviel Spaß zu empfinden. Nach diesem Erfolg war die Rutsche an diesem Tag ihr Lieblingsspielgerät. Jedes Mal, wenn sie unten ankam, freute sie sich als sei es das erste Mal.

Christina hat gelernt ihre Ängste zu überwinden. Sie hatte ein Erfolgserlebnis und Freude.

Learning Story 5.4   Christina's Learning Experience

Story 5.6, *Super Focusing Learning Powers*). 'Focusing' has two meanings, a Super Learning meaning and a technological meaning, in Learning Story 5.7, *Budding Photographer.* This Story records Samuela's interest and engagement as he develops competence with the camera.

Kieran the Book Maker

Kieran, you were so excited today when you came into the classroom from the garden. You were holding a drawing saying, "Look Mrs Kenchington, its Boxford Wood." I noticed how proud you were; you had drawn trees and the sun, just like your friend Charlie. "I can see the big tree that we play near," I said. "It's lovely!" I could see that the picture was special to you by the way you smiled at me. We have been interested in making books this week and I thought that maybe you would like to make this special picture into a book. I think that you liked this idea because you quickly found some more paper and coloured pencils and sat at the writing table with me.

You started to draw again, "Big tree, a little tree," you commented as you drew lines for the trunk and swirls for the leaves and branches. "We need a sun and rain and a rainbow." You drew a circle for the sun and added lines for the rays. You went to find more colours for your rainbow and drew the arched lines in lots of colours. We thought for a while about what else we saw at Boxford and Charlie suggested the zip wire. You drew a line from one tree to another. "I wonder how you will stick the book together?" I asked. "A stapler," you said. We found one, and you had to push very hard with both hands to make the staple come out. Just as you had finished, Miss Chamberlain came to play with you and you told her all about your book.

What learning did I see happening here?

I was really impressed with Kieran's drawing of the wood today; he had watched his friend Charlie drawing a picture and decided to draw his own. His excitement when sharing his picture with me showed just how much the real experience of Boxford Wood has influenced his learning and development. The Early Years Foundation Stage reminds us that, 'Young children require space, indoors and outdoors, where they can be active or quiet, and where they can think, dream and watch others.' It also tells us that, 'Children learn from first-hand experiences'; this is so evident for Kieran. One aspect of Kieran's 'Individual Play Plan' was for him to become confident to talk about a picture. This activity gave him the opportunity to talk to the adults within a secure context and enabled us to develop his language and vocabulary in a meaningful way.

Opportunities and possibilties

Kieran was so proud of his achievement today. I am sure he will want to repeat it. I look forward to our next visit to Boxford Woods together. Maybe Kieran would like to take some photographs and make another book to share at home. I wonder what Mummy thought of Kieran's beautiful picture.

Debbie - September

Learning Story 5.5   Kieran the Book Maker

Super FOCUSING Learning Powers

BUILDING SUPER LEARNING POWERS IS ABOUT...

Getting tamariki to think about what it takes to learn. We believe that they all have SUPER POWERS that help them to learn and we want to encourage and build on these here at Kindergarten.

If we get tamariki thinking and using their SUPER LEARNING POWERS they will be able to draw on their specific powers when they are needed.

This idea came from kaiako reading and thinking about Guy Claxton's book 'Building Learning Power'.

HAVE YOU SEEN THIS DISPLAY INSIDE KINDY?

OVER THE PAST FEW TERMS WE HAVE BEEN WORKING WITH TAMARIKI TO ENCOURAGE THEM TO USE THEIR SUPER FOCUSING POWERS:

Focusing is when you stay playing and working at one place for a long time. Focusing is a Super Learning Power because when you are learning to do something, it is important to give yourself time to think.

Super FOCUSING Learning Powers

So if you see this cape on learning stories in your child's book you'll know straight away that they have been building and using their super FOCUSING learning powers. It's important that we let them know too so they can understand this is a power they can draw on when they are learning.

TERM 3 AND 4

Learning Story 5.6　Super Focusing Learning Powers

Budding Photographer

Yesterday, Naomi got out the children's camera and this helped you get over being upset when Mum left, and kept you busy for most of the session. This morning, you told me, "Oku ou fiema'u 'ae mea koe." ("I want that" - pointing to the camera). I got the camera for you, and you were off taking pictures. You snapped a couple of pictures of me in the office, and I showed you how to review the pictures you'd taken, then you headed out to take many pictures of other tamariki, toys and the kindergarten environment. We ran out of time to print out your pictures near the end of session, so we did this the following day. You also took more pictures too.

WHAT LEARNING DID I THINK WAS HAPPENING HERE FOR SAMUELA?:

Samuela, it's cool that you're taking a real interest in our children's camera and have been taking pictures over several days now. Your interest and focus on using the camera has also been a support in helping you settle in at kindergarten on your own. So it was great to see you continuing to initiate getting out the children's camera and using it.

At Flatbush Kindergarten we encourage tamariki (children) to think about what it takes to learn and be a good learner. Kaiako (teachers) think that tamariki have SUPER POWERS that help them to learn and we want to encourage and build on these. One of these super powers is FOCUSING, and this means that a tamaiti (child) will stay playing and engaged in an area/ activity/ with particular toys/ equipment for a long time. Samuela, it was great to see you using your SUPER LEARNING POWER OF FOCUSING, and staying engaged, using the camera for a long time. Being focused is an important part of learning because it gives you time to learn and think about what you are doing and to work on goals you might have.

POSSIBILITIES AND OPPORTUNITIES:

From your keen interest I see we'll have to make sure that we keep the batteries charged up and ready to go, so you don't miss any opportunities to develop familiarity and knowledge with the camera and photography techniques :) !!!

By Akanesi   21st March

Learning Story 5.7   Budding Photographer

A number of Learning Stories in New Zealand include as indicators five actions that were described as the 'tips of icebergs' of the five curriculum strands. The indicators are: taking an interest, being involved, persisting with difficulty, expressing an idea or a feeling, and taking responsibility. These dispositions-in-action are described in some detail in the 2001 Learning Story book (Carr, 2001a). A number of research projects have built on this array of actions, finding parallel ideas – as Nikki and Susie did in Chapter 2 for the parallel 'participating and contributing' – in order to recognise episodes of value and to build on them. Table 5.1 provides five interpretations of longer term meaning-making dispositions, practices and learner identities that have enabled teachers to construct longer term analyses of the learning in their documentation (Ministry of Education, 1996, 2007; Greerton Early Childhood Centre Team; Carr and Lee, 2008; Learning Story 3.1).

Table 5.1   Longer term meaning-making dispositions, practices and learner identities: five frameworks

Te Whāriki: the national early childhood curriculum in New Zealand	Key Competencies in the New Zealand school curriculum	Learning Story framework from the original research project	A question-asking and question-exploring culture in a childcare centre	Pathways in a school
Well-being	Managing self	Being involved	Growing intelligence	RESILIENT LEARNER Managing self
Exploration	Thinking	Persevering	Playfulness	THINKER Thinking
Communication	Using language, symbols and texts	Expressing ideas	Listening dialogue	COMMUNICATOR Using language, symbols and texts
Contribution	Relating to others	Taking responsibility	Real work	CARING CITIZEN Relating to others
Belonging	Participating and contributing	Taking an interest	Continuity	Participating and contributing

The Opportunities for Learning Stories and Portfolios to Construct Continuities and to Make them Visible

There are several ways in which continuities can be deliberately constructed and made visible in Learning Stories and portfolios: inside the story, in the analysis of the learning, in the planning section of the Learning Story, in a sequence of episodes or photographs gathered together, and in conversations about the Learning Stories with the learner or a group.

Making Continuity Visible: Inside the Story

Often Learning Stories include continuity inside the story, by putting together a number of shorter episodes to tell a longer story, as the teachers of Evie (in *Evie Comes Prepared*, Chapter 4) did, or by referring to the past (*That was Then! This is Now!*, Box 5.3).

Box 5.3

Jo writes a story in Keira's portfolio, entitled 'That was then! This is now!'

Only two weeks ago I wrote a story about Keira exploring the challenge of the trapeze bar with the support of her friend Olivia. Today, as I wandered outside, there I saw Keira hanging upside down, with her feet in the air and a smile a mile wide. Quickly grabbing the camera I was able to capture some of Keira's acrobatics mid flight.

Making Continuity Visible: in the Analysis of the Learning

Keira's portfolio describes and annotates her explorations and learning over time. Her portfolio begins with a Welcome story, written by Jo, her Primary Caregiver who comments that: 'We will begin many learning journeys together.' Three-and-a-half years later, Lorraine writes a Learning Story about

Keira teaching a friend to do a difficult manoeuvre on the geo-gym. In the analysis of the learning, Lorraine added that:

> Keira, I have seen you work like this ever since you were a baby, pushing yourself to the limits of your ability, always looking for the next opportunity to test yourself. Then with effort and practice honing your skills. These are such great learning dispositions, Keira, to take into life.

Lorraine writes a 'summary' story for Jackson's portfolio (see Learning Story 5.8 *Jackson's Investigations Keep Getting More and More Complex!*). It includes a still photo from video footage of Jackson as a baby experimenting with water flow at the end of a hose, and ending with 'Jackson's CV':

> *Jackson's CV.* Now at 4, Jackson is the CEO of a thriving, experimental company of engineers who passionately donate their time and effort to the interests of pushing technology beyond current known limits.
>
> *Future Aspirations.* The skills required in the 21st century are as yet unknown because the jobs haven't been invented yet. The dispositions required to be the inventors of those jobs are already being practised by Jackson. Watch this space!

Making Continuity Visible: in the Planning Section of a Learning Story

Julie traces the development of Scarlett's koru patterns in two adjacent Learning Stories (see Learning Story 5.9 *Scarlett's Koru, Butterfly and Flower Book*). In the first of these she notes that Scarlett is doing some great experimentation with the koru shape, using it to make patterns. She suggests that Scarlett might take the designs into other art media. Two weeks later Scarlett is drawing a sculpted koru and a series of koru that she labels as members of her family 'Mummy', 'Daddy' and 'all the kids'. Then she makes two screen prints of the koru patterns. A photo shows another child holding the paper for her while she cuts out the patterns, and one of the completed screen prints.

Making Continuity Visible: in a Sequence of Episodes or Photographs Gathered Together

In the following sequence of episodes, written by Cathie, Bayley's classroom teacher, Learning Stories recorded moments of progress for Bayley as he chose the book corner as a place of comfort, became interested in books, recognised some of the skills associated with book reading, and participated in social interactions around reading (see Box 5.4). The teacher's primary intent was Bayley's emergent literacy, but the storying enabled a contextualised account, recording some significant aspects of the facilitating environment. This sequence was accompanied by photographs, not included here but clearly referred to in the text.

JACKSON'S INVESTIGATIONS KEEP GETTING MORE AND MORE COMPLEX!

Presently, Jackson's work revolves around Hot Wheels experiments, supported by impressive motorways that take many hours each day to construct, as more and more complex designs are built and dismantled.

Jackson's investigations began a long time ago....

It seems to me that ever since I met Jackson as a very young baby, he has had 'investigation' on his mind. His curiosity on that first morning, as he sat on the grass for over an hour playing with the hose, was limitless. He was testing the water-flow by putting his finger in the end of the hose and releasing it. I've seen that little video often and I am always so intrigued by the effort and practice, the complete intent to test and re-test, as Jackson built theories around how the

pressure from his finger changed the way the water squirted. Such determination for someone so young! If ever I want to recall an incident that epitomises Te Whāriki's aspiration statement "...that children are competent and capable..." it is this one, particularly when referring to babies. What was important then and remains so now for teachers/kaiako, is a burning desire to support children to find the things that captivate their interests. When we set up an

environment that is full of intrigue and allows space and time for children's investigations, we generate a setting that supports children to 'learn to love to learn'. Their research is driven by dispositions that keep them involved, setting and solving problems and building social spaces to test their theories. This is just what Jackson continually does. A traditional Te Ao Māori method of carrying a baby is a metaphor that describes for me the way a learning setting might

How do we get from hose to block building extravaganzas?

Jackson can tell you – practice and effort, driven by a disposition to be curious and a willingness to test and re-test to reach your goals. These are internally motivated dispositions that can be shifted from one context to another and allow learners and learning to thrive!

JACKSON AS A YOUNG EXPERIMENTER AT EMMETT STREET

(Continued)

(Continued)

truly support individual children to explore their world. A blanket was woven, made from the harakeke plant to provide strength and filled with albatross feathers for warmth. The blanket (te whatu pokeka) was pliable, so as the baby grew, it took on the shape of the child, rather than the child fitting into a predetermined shape. I love this image as it relates to the learning culture we have, for so long now, tried to grow here at Greerton. Jackson <u>so</u> shapes his own learning, and more and more now he is drawing other children into his experiments as this passionate learner excites others to become involved. The latest movies I've taken show this social side to Jackson, as his inclusive leadership enables a huge experimental culture around Hot Wheels cars and the building of motorways to thrive. He now has a range of friends who are 'on the job' with him as engineers, co-constructing these technological marvels. He has a band of 'apprentices' who range from avid watchers of the 'experts in action', to the tentative contributor. That is the hallmark of learning the skills which they have first of all observed so closely.

This is a tuakana teina relationship, where an older child assists a younger, less experienced child, enabling them to participate and grow their skills alongside experts.

Jackson models such passion for experimentation, for testing and re-testing and does so in a way that is fascinating to watch. One particular afternoon recently I was in awe as seven actively involved boys

worked together in the area just by the office where we currently have situated the blocks. As these boys weaved in and around each other, building and rebuilding, cars flew frenetically down the tracks on test runs and shot off in various directions. The watchers were present around the edges and action abounded everywhere. Yet, all I witnessed was unified harmony. I wish the country could be run with such clarity of purpose! Jackson was the CEO of a major company, with colleagues dedicated to a vision based on stretching their imaginations and working hard

to reach their goals. He has developed a community of learners or what might also be described as a 'kaupapa whānau': a community drawn together by a common purpose and a commitment to action. So, Jackson is in our community here at Greerton, being a learner and being a teacher; leading, collaborating, pushing the boundaries of design and workmanship. What a fabulous place to be – at the edge of learning, wanting more and prepared to risk failure as a way to learn! Kia kaha, Jackson.

From Your friend, Lorraine

The work in its infancy - my, how the buildings have expanded in complexity since February!

FUTURE ASPIRATIONS

THE SKILLS REQUIRED IN THE 21ST CENTURY ARE AS YET UNKNOWN BECAUSE THE JOBS HAVEN'T BEEN INVENTED YET. THE DISPOSITIONS REQUIRED TO BE THE INVENTORS OF THOSE JOBS ARE ALREADY BEING PRACTICED BY JACKSON. WATCH THIS SPACE!

JACKSON'S CV

NOW AGED 4, JACKSON IS THE CEO OF A THRIVING, EXPERIMENTAL COMPANY OF ENGINEERS, WHO PASSIONATELY DONATE THEIR TIME AND EFFORT TO THE INTERESTS OF PUSHING TECHNOLOGY BEYOND CURRENT KNOWN LIMITS.

Learning Story 5.8   Jackson's Investigations Keep Getting More and More Complex!

Scarlett's Koru, Butterfly and Flower Book

I have noticed over the last while that Scarlett loves drawing the koru shape.

One time, as Scarlett was drawing her koru, she said to me, "I'm Māori." I am sure that drawing the koru helps her link to her cultural heritage and identity.

Scarlett watched George make a book with me using the spiral binder and she wanted to make one too.

She was very confident in how she approached the task of binding her book.

I would like to offer Scarlett the opportunity to develop her interest in the koru shape further.

Julie, 21st October

Scarlett's Amazing Koru Art

I asked Scarlett if she would like to draw a picture of a koru to screen print and showed her my little koru sculpture.

Scarlett produced several drawings of the sculpture - 36 in all! "The big one is the Mummy one, and the Daddy and all the kids." - "it looks like you're drawing your whānau."

Then she made a couple of fantastic screen prints.

Scarlett was 100% committed to her project and absolutely absorbed in her work. Cutting out the shape was tricky but she attacked the challenge with great gusto.

Tomorrow I will ask Scarlett if she wants to build on her work, maybe using pen or paint, she might like to do an over print, we'll see.

Julie, 8th November

Learning Story 5.9 Scarlett's Koru, Butterfly and Flower Book

Box 5.4

Bayley manages self, relates to others, and approaches New Zealand Curriculum English Level 1

A series of stories about Bayley from March to July describe his growing interest in reading.

March. Since the beginning of the year, Bayley is attending more and more and is becoming increasingly familiar with and comfortable in, our classroom. His Teacher Aide told me this morning that he was very excited to be returning to school after the Easter break. Today when Bayley entered the classroom he headed straight to the couch in the library corner. This is his favourite area of the room. As you can see from the photos he likes to make himself comfortable! The book in his hand is a favourite that he picks out from the book shelf most days. He doesn't open the book but enjoys looking at the cover.

June. Bayley enjoys the class library corner. It is a favourite place for him to head to, especially if he is a little tired and needs some time out. He usually picks out the one book to hold that has been a favourite since he started school. The red cover seems very appealing to him. Yesterday, during lunchtime, he discovered a new book while he was having a quiet time in the library corner with his teacher aide. Today, at reading time, he chose the same book from the bookshelf, made himself comfortable on the bean bag and settled down to enjoy the book. He began at the start of the book and turned the pages by himself, looking carefully at the pictures on each page. Sometimes he turned the book upside down to look at a picture but then turned it round again to turn to the next page.

July. Today, after lunch, Bayley demonstrated that he is aware of some of the routines at school. He came in and went to his schedule, with the help of his aide. He then looked at the picture of reading in class, took it off, and peered around to look at the reading corner where the children share books, showing that he understood where this activity takes place. He was then approached by two girls who wanted to read a book with him. They all made themselves comfortable and shared a couple of books with Bayley. He was engaged in their books, following their instructions to look at the pages and sometimes turning pages himself. Occasionally he lost focus, but they directed his attention back to the books with success. The book that held his attention for the longest time was his own book 'I am Bayley'.

Charleeh-Blu's development with drawing is reflected in a significant chain of five stories written and gathered together by Akanesi, Joanne and Naomi (see Learning Story 5.10, *Charleeh-Blu Stories*).

Exploring drawing with block animals

Charleeh, you joined me and several other tamariki this afternoon, drawing animals using the wooden block animals for inspiration and templates. What I thought was wonderful was that you showed an important disposition – characteristic of a good learner – that you were eager and open to trying something new. This learning behaviour is something I'd already noticed when you started, but it's great to see you appear curious and eager to learn and try new things all the time. I hope to keep an eye out for more examples of this.

Written by Akanesi 19th June

"Aunty, I draw my crocodile".

Charleeh-Blu's house

Written by Joanne 15th March

Charleeh-Blu had the intention to do a large painting. As she started this she said, "I don't know what I want to paint." However, she got the brushes and poised over the paper, deep in concentration. Using the light blue, she made a square, then she drew lines around the outside. Next came the purple line and some strokes, then the red, which she filled in beside the purple to make more squares, and then came the dots in the middle. She was very focused when she did this painting. When the painting was completed she said, "This is a large house, it has lots of windows, a door and walls." Later, when talking to Lynette, she said it was her 'school'.

What Learning was happening here:
Charleeh-Blu thought about what she was going to paint and spent time working out how she was going to achieve this. She chose her colours carefully.
It was really good to see you had thought about your picture in detail.

Opportunities and possibilities:
As Charleeh-Blu grows, she is developing some amazing ideas, which, in turn, is giving her the confidence to set her own learning.

Drawings for our Birds

Written by Akanesi 3rd November

Today, after looking at the blackbirds my uncle brought in from the tree they cut down, and on hearing that they were not faring so well, you had a beautiful thought: to show them you care, you would draw them a picture. This inspired a whole group of other tamariki to join in making drawings for our birds.

Where is their mum?

(Continued)

(Continued)

As the birds were going downhill very fast, I thought we'd take them to the SPCA. To give you time to say goodbye, and to share your work, we brought everyone to mat time so you could do this. You also suggested singing the birds a song (we did so quietly, so as not to frighten them).

Your question about where their mother was highlights how you were thinking about their situation and maybe, just a bit, putting yourself in their situation. This is an important part of developing social skills and empathy and sympathy for fellow human beings and other creatures.

What empathy you showed today, Charleeh-Blu, in wanting to check up on our birds and bringing them a picture to cheer them up! We talked about how they were away from their mum and were probably missing her. Thank you for also being a leader today and inspiring other tamariki to show their caring for other creatures through creating artwork for them.

Thank you Charleeh-Blu

Charleeh-Blu, I wanted to thank you for all the lovely creations you have made for me! Here are a few photos of just some of what you have made for me. I have recently written a story about your wonderful caring nature, Charleeh-Blu, and how you are so often making things for others and I wanted to say a big thank you to you!

Written by Naomi - 22nd March

Practice makes Perfect!

Written by Akanesi 23rd March

Charleeh-Blu, you always blow me away with your thoughtfulness in making pictures for others including me, other kaiako, your friends and whānau! Today was no exception. You brought over a colourful picture, and said that it was for all of the kaiako, but that you wanted to hang it (off the door handle).

When I asked you to tell me about your picture, you explained about the whale (see next page for comments), and about how you have practised and practised to be able to draw it.

(Continued)

(Continued)

What learning did I see happening here for Charleeh-Blu?
Charleeh-Blu, the arts of drawing, collage, writing and painting are all continuing to be a big interest for you. Talking to Scott the other day, he said that you love to draw and paint every day and I replied, I could see you becoming an artist and he totally agreed. It was interesting because he and Jules were looking at getting you the very special birthday present (a painting easel) to support and encourage your interest.

Charleeh-Blu, it was awesome to hear you again link practice to learning to get better at drawing more detailed whales. It's taken a while, Charleeh-Blu - learning can and does take time and practice - however, your words "...Because I PRACTISE and PRACTISE. Because I couldn't do it at home. And then I PRACTISE and PRACTISE...now I can draw a whale" reflect that you really seem to understand and have internalised your learning with Super PRACTISING Learning Powers.

Opportunities and Possibilities: I know that you will find as much enjoyment in seeing and reading your stories as the kaiako have in documenting them, so maybe we could talk about what else you'd like to see in here.

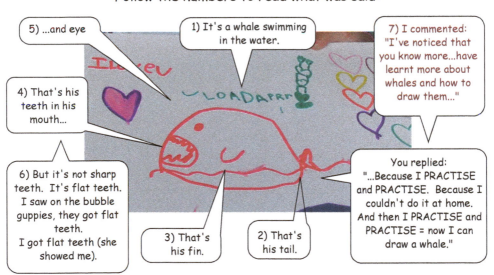

Learning Story 5.10   Charleeh-Blu Stories

Making Continuity Visible: in Conversations about the Learning Stories with the Learner or a Group

As we saw in Chapter 3, conversations provide opportunities for students to explain their own meaning and enable the teacher to emphasise the connections between episodes and to the learning valued at the centre. They also provide an opportunity for learners to recognise and re-cognise portfolios as tracers of the learning journey. We met Isabella in the previous chapter, making a necklace for her grandmother. Isabella had spent many months exploring design and its challenges in mosaic and bead media. In the following conversation she is shifting her focus to using this knowledge and skill to make things for others. In a discussion with Kim (a teacher) about one of her recent Learning Stories she described her plan for mosaics:

> *Kim*: [points to a photo] Did you make this for anyone special?
> *Isabella*: [looks at teacher, smiling] Um, I made it for my sister! [pauses and then nods] I have to make one for my Mummy [counting on her hand] and my Daddy as well.
> *K*: Do you?
> *I*: I've got two things to make. [holds up both hands with two fingers pointing up on each hand]
> *K*: Two things. Is that your plan?
> *I*: Yep.
> *K*: That's a good plan. [Isabella smiles]

She does indeed complete two more mosaics during the following month. When children returned to their interests and their favourite activities, they were always implicitly making connections between the past and the present, and stories often capture this continuity of interest, as Devya's portfolio did in Chapter 4.

Concluding Comments

We have found the notion of a portfolio as housing 'significant chains of episodes' to be a useful one. The image that comes to mind is that of the paperchains that we used to make as children, and for our children, on special occasions. But it might be helpful to think of these as 're-negotiable' chains, since we often re-cognise what appears to have been going on some time after the documented event or for different audiences. A *re-negotiable chain of learning episodes* describes an apparent coherence of learning: a sustained strengthening in what appears to be the same or a similar topic, skill, learning disposition or cultural practice. Teachers who know the children well will recognise the many chains of meaning-making in any one child's portfolio, and their commentary will make this learning visible (Giudici, Rinaldi and Krechevsky, 2001). Sometimes the topic of interest to the child is not clear. Kim wrote a story about her conversation with Tominiko, a conversation that might be difficult to allocate to a chain of learning episodes. It does however illustrate the way in which a portfolio acts as a material object that carries significant information, for Tominiko, of this figured world (his kindergarten) and its possibilities. It began as follows:

This morning Tominiko and I were sitting together on the couch having a chat. 'Kim, you have a boyfriend' he said to me. 'I do,' I replied, 'His name is Steve'. 'I know' said Tominiko, 'I see him'. I thought about this comment and wondered where Tominiko might have seen Steve. 'Oh' I said 'Have you seen Steve when he comes to help cook the barbecue?' 'Yes, and he in my book. You wait, I show you' and off he ran to find his portfolio [and then began a conversation about his jigsaw puzzle prowess, his Spiderman stories – and Kim's boyfriend (in stories the teachers had contributed about their holidays)].

As Chapter 1 argues, a learning journey will often be a mingling and merging of dispositional and disciplinary (subject-based) elements and a portfolio will trace the meaning-making dispositions as well as the mastery of challenges in a particular skill or knowledge area. The record of Bayley's learning in Box 5.4 was an example. In the 2001 Learning Story book, the notion of foregrounding and backgrounding was useful: sometimes the inclination, sometimes the knowledge and skill, and sometimes the sensitivity to occasion is foregrounded. In Chapter 2, Danielle had mastered the skill of swinging herself, while at the same time recognising the role in learning of being taught: 'You just teached me! … Remember?' In Chapter 5 Zac had mastered the art of writing STOP, and recognised that he had learned this from a model in a workplace. Documenting these minglings and mergers provides challenges for teachers because learning and learning environments are complex. Edwin Hutchins (1996) had introduced the notion of 'cognition in the wild', referring to the interdisciplinary nature of cognition in activities outside the laboratory, and we saw in Chapter 2 that David Perkins and colleagues at Harvard's Project Zero programme described learning environments as 'wildernesses' of 'vaguely marked and ill-defined occasions for thoughtful engagement' (Perkins, Tishman, Ritchhart, Donis and Andrade, 2000: 270). González, Moll and Amanti (2005: 1) writing about the Funds of Knowledge programme (see Chapter 4 and Chapter 1, note 4) expressed the view that: 'well-grounded and illuminating analytical points flow only from bringing concepts into a relationship with the messiness of ordinary life, somehow recorded'. They say that this messiness is 'the everyday practices that we attempt to theorize, practices that are at times emergent, perhaps counter intuitive, and sometimes opaque' (ibid.: 1). Chapter 6 will continue this discussion about continuity and complexity, to consider a final theme and consequence of Learning Stories: a mapping of the increasingly complex ways in which learners appropriate knowledges and dispositions in local contexts.

Notes

1 Jay Lemke provides the commentary for a special issue of the *Journal of the Learning Sciences* on rethinking methodology in the learning sciences in which the idea of continuity residing in 'networks of action-relevant episodes' is introduced. Perhaps *action-relevant episodes* have some kin with Learning Stories. Sasha Barab, Kenneth Hay and Lisa Yamagata-Lynch's paper on this topic develops a complex way in which episodes in a classroom research project can be linked by time, practices, resources and people. They comment that:

a central methodological concern in our research has been how to capture the trajectory of learning as it unfolds over the semester-long courses. In other words, rather than describing students' ready-made knowledge at the end of the course we have been interested in tracking knowing in the making as the course unfolds. In fact, from our situated perspective, the notion of knowledge existing as a thing that can be assessed apart from the learning context becomes suspect. (2001: 64)

Their approach begins with the analysing of classroom experiences into 'chunks' or 'action-relevant episodes'. Emphasising learning as participation and relationship, a theme in this book, they add that:

in our conception, knowing about and learning are simply different ways of describing the dynamics of evolving participation. Becoming knowledgeably skillful, from this perspective, is characterized by an individual's increasing potential to build and transform relations with the (material, psychological, and social) world. (Ibid.: 66)

2   This Super Learner Hero project has resonance with a book entitled *Learning Power Heroes* from the *Building Learning Power* programme in England. Guy Claxton (2009) wrote the following in a foreword to that book, emphasising teachers as learning 'heroes':

(Children) learn to learn in the way their parents, carers and teachers learn. If they grow up around people who love to debate round the dinner table they will imbibe the habits, rules and pleasures of debating. If they watch adults being experimental, inquisitive and tenacious in their learning these habits will rub off too. If their role models have no time for ideas, or become angry the minute their efforts are frustrated, that too is what they will learn. So we must be careful to be at our learning best around young children, especially if they like or admire us, for their 'heroes' are the people whose habits they will find the most contagious. (p. 1)

We might contemplate the notion that teachers who document learning in stories, consulting with the children and families along the way, are also providing role models for the learners in their classrooms and early childhood settings. Children observe the adults as they write notes, gather data and take photographs about learning episodes. The adults are modelling an interest in learning and are focused and curious, keen to talk about significant episodes and to share their noticing: they may model a passion for a wide range of interesting outcomes and they value and respect the viewpoints of families. Where it is possible to construct a Learning Story with the learner they are modelling collaborative and purposeful literacy. These learning habits can become contagious too.

Appropriating Knowledges and Learning Dispositions in a Range of Increasingly Complex Ways

Box 6.1

(W)e noticed that Kayla would often revisit her own portfolio and those of other tamariki [children] whilst sitting on a chair. She revisited her portfolio daily and would often carry it around. Her favourite place was that green chair. Her portfolio was her cuddly blanket and it never went anywhere without her and she never went anywhere without it. ... We also noticed that Kayla used her portfolio to build relationships with people, including visitors to the centre. She often would persevere with gestures etc. to ensure that we understood what she was trying to communicate with her limited vocabulary. (Thelma, teacher: Reflections on Kayla early in the year she was turning four years of age)

This chapter builds on the discussion so far about the complex ways in which learners appropriate knowledges and dispositions and the ways in which Learning Stories can document and assist with this complicated task. The word 'appropriation' is used in the way that James Wertsch explained it in Chapter 1: to make something one's own. In that chapter, too, we defined 'appropriating knowledges and learning dispositions in a range of increasingly complex ways' using the words of Na'ilah Suad Nasir and her colleagues as 'the specific ways of conceptualising, representing, evaluating and engaging with the world'. Chapter 4 described the role of Learning Stories and portfolios in documenting and constructing the learning journey across *settings, places* or *communities*. This chapter is about documenting and constructing the learning journey across varied *modes and languages* for communicating, meaning-making, conceptualising and representing. Carey Jewitt (2008) commented on a link between multimodal representation and 'remixing and remaking genres':

> Multimodal representation and globalization are close companions, providing new foundations for processes of remixing and remaking genres and modal resources in ways that produce new forms of global and commercial processes. These in turn are constantly personalized, appropriated, and remade in local workplaces, communities, and institutions. (p. 243) ... Multimodality attends to meaning as it is made through the situated configurations across image, gesture, gaze, body posture, sound, writing, music, speech, and so on. From a multimodal perspective, image, action, and so forth are referred to as *modes*, as organized sets of semiotic resources for making meaning. (p. 246)

In Chapter 3 Toby had exclaimed, 'I'm a genius in my head and a genius in my hands!' and we had noted that Zeb, Emma and Thenusan's story-telling began with drawing and block construction. This is not a stage of development to be completed; a sociocultural account of learning sees it as the development of a repertoire of modes and practices that will be available over the life span, and, as Seymour Papert (1993: 151) said of concrete thinking expressed in gesture, movement, dance, drawing and construction: 'Children do it, people in Pacific and African villages do it, and so do most sophisticated people in Paris or Geneva.' These modes begin to develop in the early years, and the disposition to enjoy them, practise them and to find them helpful does, too. The 2001 Learning Story book (Carr, 2001a: 14) quoted Papert's (1980, 1993) early work on computers and education to make this point:

> Seymour Papert (1993) emphasised action and 'concreteness' and criticised what he called the 'perverse commitment to moving as quickly as possible from the concrete to the abstract' (p. 143) at school. He put it nicely when he suggested that 'formal methods are on tap, not on top'. (p. 146)

In this chapter we illustrate the role of Learning Stories in shaping this multimodality in two ways. The first is a recognition of the new modes of meaning-making, conceptualising and representing in the digital revolution over the last ten years, and a consideration of the ways in which Learning Stories have tried to keep up with this. The second is the recognition that chains of learning episodes may be re-negotiated, depending on which mode or language (in the widest sense) is highlighted. The focus of interest for the teacher, researcher or parent will be what is noticed and recognised and receives a response.

New Modes of Meaning-making, Conceptualising and Representing

Learning Stories have now participated in the new digital technologies in three ways: transforming the ways in which Learning Stories can be constructed, tracing children's Information Communications Technology (ICT) learning journeys, and emphasising the value of image-based ways of thinking.

Transforming the Ways in Which Learning Stories can be Constructed

Learning Stories have developed alongside the first explosion of ICTs as accessible tools for information-gathering and documenting children's learning. We both remember our excitement at using the Polaroid camera in the early research that led to Learning Stories, and we both recognise that ICTs have changed the way we can collect and process data, and the way we think and write. The difference between this book and the 2001 Learning Story book is a case in point. We can in this book illustrate our ideas using colour photographs, and the images do a lot of the work of telling the story. It is the same for Learning Stories; the examples of Learning Stories in a section on 'diverse assessment formats' in the 2001 Learning Story book (Carr, 2001a: 144–50) include stories written by hand on a formatted sheet, and photographs were attached with some difficulty and well after the event – after the film had been sent away to be developed. Learning Stories are often, now, image-based. Reading them is different. Teachers are placing photographs on DVDs as slide shows, sometimes adding sound – music or commentary – and these DVDs are placed in children's portfolios. A slide show of Nathan's play is in his portfolio, available for revisiting at kindergarten or at home. Jane, one of the teachers, commented:

Watching this slide show of Nathan's, I have realised that the putting together of the slides was also an occasion of re-visiting. Once I had put the slides in order, Nathan watched them, and as he told the story to go with each one he commented that he'd like to do it again. This was recorded as part of his story, with the result that every time he re-visits his slide show, he is reminded of what he did, that he wanted to do it again then, and this sometimes prompts him to do it again now.

Ten years ago, Wendy Lee, Karen Ramsey and Ann Hatherly commented:

An area of great interest ... to us has been how ICT is assisting teachers with documentation ... Digital video and still cameras used in conjunction with

> computers have been pivotal in providing easier access to documentation and the curriculum, especially for children and their families. This applies particularly when a Learning Story contains a series of photos illustrating 'work in progress' as opposed to a one-off 'tourist shot' of the finished product. (Lee, Hatherly and Ramsey, 2002: 10)

Karen R. later tells the story of the interconnection between the kindergarten's digital and assessment practices journeys (in Carr, Hatherly, Lee and Ramsey, 2003):

> *Term 1 2001*. Last year we had made greater use of photographs in documenting children's learning. This meant the children's learning stories had meaning for them and they could re-visit and share their experiences with their friends – very motivating for oral, visual and written literacy. Photographs were also extremely powerful for our families and especially those with English as an additional language. During Term 4 I had regularly talked to the committee about the need for a digital camera. (p. 199)

The kindergarten held a Monster Garage sale and raised enough for a digital camera. But they didn't have a computer. In Term 2 they applied to be part of a pilot programme to explore the possibilities of computers in kindergartens. They were selected, and Karen wrote in Term 2 of 2001:

> We had worked hard developing our assessment system during the past year and were passionate about documenting our children's learning. Having a computer and digital camera meant we could take our assessment system to a higher level! (p. 200)

Chapter 4 included some of this 'higher level': the *Temple Design* story (Learning Story 4.8) from Devya's portfolio illustrated his referring to the pictures from a website to inform his block-building. His portfolio also included a DVD of his work, and Learning Stories were prepared as wall displays and PowerPoints for groups of children to revisit and plan together. Included here is another Devya story, *The Mandir*, which describes Devya explaining and sharing ideas with other children as they watch a DVD of a temple in England, and Devya then referencing the images on the screen to make more temple drawings.

Tracing Children's Learning Journeys

By now, even very young children are co-authoring their own Learning Stories by taking photographs as well as by dictating texts, and they are making PowerPoints, books and movies (Carr, Lee and Jones, 2009: 20). In the Mandir story, Devya combines a computer image with drawing, and the children's work with ICTs is often included in a portfolio as a chain of learning episodes.

The Mandir

24th November
Karen

For quite some time I have been meaning to share the Mandir DVD with Devya. This is the temple I visited when I was in England. Kellen and Isabella joined us and we settled down, ready with anticipation to see what we would see.

Ever since I shared my photos with Devya, he was very keen to see an inside view of the Mandir. In particular, he was very keen to see what the gods looked like. We had visited the Mandir website quite a few times and had seen pictures of the gods, but still hadn't seen how they actually looked in the temple.

When the first image appeared on the screen, Devya's eyes lit up and sparkled with excitement. He heard the chanting begin and bowed down when he saw the image of the gods. The narrator started talking and we listened to the story of how the temple was built. Throughout the story, Devya explained points to his friends and shared his ideas and thoughts with us.

Devya often commented on the beauty of the temple and the gods and was especially pleased when he saw Krishna.

When the DVD was nearly finished, Devya disappeared and soon returned with paper and pens. He took up his position again and began to draw, totally absorbed with the task at hand.

(Continued)

(Continued)

Friends came and went and Devya continued to draw. When the DVD had finished, he requested to watch it again, glancing up from his work every now and again to check for detail.

When Devya had finished his drawings, he explained the first picture was too small to fit the gods in the temple so he had turned the page and began again.

Devya explained this picture was the temple in the beginning and the picture below is the finished temple at the opening party.

The DVD continued to play until the end of session and Devya continued to draw.

What learning do I think is happening for Devya?

We all know about Devya's passion for drawing and in particular drawing his ideas and thoughts about the Hindu gods. It is fair to say that Devya draws every day and is very keen to share his thinking with his friends and teachers. When I had the opportunity to visit the Mandir in Needson, England, the first person I thought of was Devya and his passion. This has inspired me to learn more and deepen my knowledge of the Hindu religion.

The Mandir DVD deepened our knowledge and provided the answers to the questions Devya had been asking. What did it look like inside?

It came as no surprise that Devya would begin to draw what he saw. It was more a matter of when would he decide to begin to represent his ideas through his pictures. Devya's pictures are very complex and the detail is amazing. This tells me he is thinking deeply about what he sees and is confident in his own ability to turn his ideas and thoughts into a picture. He is evaluating his work and sometimes decides to begin again.

Devya is also exploring mathematical concepts through his drawing, concepts such as size, symmetry and patterns. Devya can draw in a two dimensional or three dimensional perspective and sometimes uses both styles in his pictures.

I look forward to listening to Devya's stories as he continues to develop his ideas and working theories and his passion.

Learning Story 6.1 The Mandir

There is a story entitled 'The Photographer at Work' that we included in *Kei Tua o te Pae* (Carr, Lee and Jones, 2009, 20: 18–19). It is a story about Nissa who decides to document a learning episode for a group Learning Story, as she has seen the teachers do (Box 6.2).

Box 6.2

The photographer at work: a Learning Story (abridged)

Robyn L. (a teacher) and a group of children are cooking pikelets, at the request of one of the children. Robyn writes:

I wanted to take photographs but I couldn't because I was just too busy. I looked up and there was Nissa, standing with the camera switched on and ready to use. She began to take photographs and I was so grateful, thinking to myself that Jane had asked her to document our cooking. But Jane looked surprised and said that she hadn't asked Nissa to get the camera. Astonished, I realised that Nissa had gone and got the camera on her own and had begun to take photos. She zoomed the lens in and out, clicking the button, making sure that

she photographed not just the people but the process as well. She took the photos from many different angles. I didn't have to think about photos, I just trusted her to document the process and she did. Thanks Nissa.

A few days later Robyn noticed Nissa recording her house construction.

Emphasising the Value of Image-based Ways of Thinking

Gunther Kress points out in his book on *Literacy in the new media age* (2003) that 'the world narrated' is a different world to 'the world depicted and displayed' (p. 2). He adds that:

> New forms of reading, when texts *show the world* rather than *tell the world* have consequences for the relations between makers and remakers of meaning (writers and readers, image-makers and viewers). (p. 140)

Learning Stories might be said to work across these two worlds: a world *narrated* in a Learning Story – telling a story, using a printed text – has also included the world *depicted and displayed* – photographs, PowerPoints, slide shows and DVDs. The 'subjects' in a chain of episodes are often the strengthening of one or more of the image-based modes of representation or conceptual thinking: the drawing or the three-dimensional construction. Some time after Lucy and Elizabeth had constructed a bridge from cellotape (the Sticky Bridge in Chapter 3), Lucy constructed a bridge from clay and the teacher took a photograph. This became part of a story line about Lucy's growing repertoire of three-dimensional construction modes (see photo).

A number of photographs by Jesse are attached here; they are part of a series of what the teachers describe as 'photographic scrap-booking'. Marianne, the teacher, comments in the Learning Story about Jesse's work:

As I downloaded your photos with you I noticed an interesting series of photos of the coloured balancing blocks. I was reminded of your previous series of photos of the mosaic squares and thought that they really convey your interest in detail and design. Again your perspective was looking down on these blocks and included your feet, which add an interesting dimension.

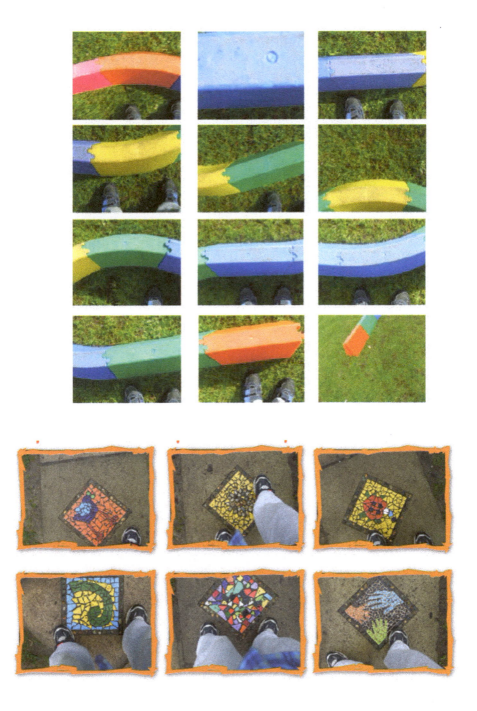

Jo Colbert was the first early childhood teacher to become an e-Fellow in a programme funded by the Ministry of Education, enabling her to explore e-learning in an early childhood centre for a term. She became interested in the implications and opportunities for the definition of 'literacy' when children can record a story without writing – enabling literacy to be woven into the lives of children in an authentic way. She explored the ways of extending the story telling interests of children through the use of ICT, working with five four-year-old children and the teachers. One of the children was Casper, who made a slide show using KidPix and who very quickly picked up the steps needed to insert photos into an iMovie show. Jo reported:

> By mid-June I had introduced a USB microphone at kindergarten. Casper wanted to have a go at using it and asked me if he could sing a song. He had a love of funny noises and made-up words; using the microphone could record many of these, interweaving them with the words of his song. (Colbert, 2006: 3)

One of the teachers at the centre, Nadine, wrote the following comment in a Learning Story about the process: 'The following week Casper asked if he could tell a story into the microphone, which I say "Yes" to, and before I get to the laptop Casper is there with GarageBand open and a track elected to begin to tell his story' (Colbert, 2006: 3). In one of his stories (about a Mr Boing Boing) Casper told his story, added some drumbeats and supported the story with his own drawings that he had photographed and added. He made this into a QuickTime movie that he took home.

A Recognition that Chains of Learning Episodes can be Re-negotiated, Depending on which Mode or Language is Highlighted

In the Reggio Emilia programmes in northern Italy, symbol systems are described as 'one hundred languages' for making meaning and communicating. Carlina Rinaldi writes about listening 'to the hundred, the thousand languages, symbols and codes we use to express ourselves and communicate, and with which life expresses itself and communicates to those who know how to listen' (Rinaldi, 2006: 65). We are indebted to the Reggio Children projects and people and to their collaborative partners at Harvard's Project Zero for making learning visible in so many thoughtful and amazing ways (Giudici, Rinaldi and Krechevsky, 2001)[1].

This chapter introduced Kayla, who was developing some of the hundred languages for making meaning and communicating, and we consider how a portfolio and Learning Stories can act as material objects that document and support the learning, and how at one centre a growing expertise and curiosity is distributed across a wide range of modes and 'languages'. In the year before she went on to school, Kayla's languages developed as she deepened her knowledge of and communication about koru patterns (of significance in Māori art; see

Scarlett's art work in Chapter 5) and tā moko (tattoo) and their cultural contexts across modes: oral language; pictures and photographs (in her portfolio, books, on the Internet and displayed on the wall); carvings of historical and cultural significance; tā moko on bodies as well as in photographs, drawing, painting, writing, claywork and a collaborative construction. At the same time, the teachers provide examples of her growing confidence, curiosity, animation, perseverance, socialisation and interest. Thelma writes about the early development of this interest at a celebration at the centre of the 1840 signing of a Treaty (Te Tiriti o Waitangi) between the Māori and the Crown:

> The Waitangi celebrations brought in many visitors, and Laurie stood out because of his tā moko (tattoo) and his vibrant personality. Kayla sat staring at his moko for a good twenty minutes, and this began an amazing metamorphosis for Kayla. … Over the ensuing months Kayla moved from a position of aloneness to being the centre of a community of learners, from the periphery to the centre. How wonderful to see this emerging over the weeks. Kayla developed a curiosity and a desire for knowledge. She became more animated and other children sought her out for the knowledge and expertise that she was acquiring. … She became an expert, not only in drawing the koru but in accessing books, the internet, drawing kowhaiwhai rafter patterns, marae, puzzles etc. She made connections between tā moko and her mother's tattoo, and Laurie's tā moko and that on a carving. In her persevering, her practical skills, her language and her socialisation grew stronger. Other children also recognised this and sought her help from the funds of knowledge that she had built up. … She has now become an enabler for other children. (Thelma, teacher)

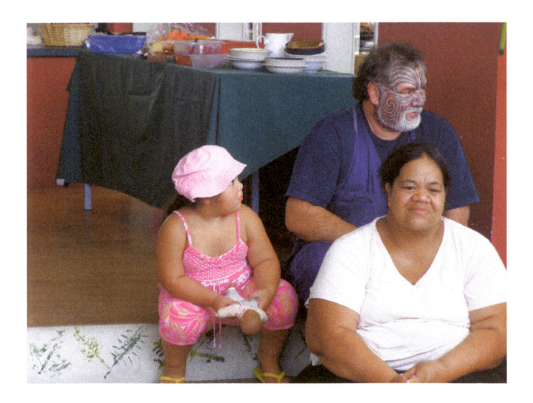

The story is briefly told in Box 6.3, from Learning Story excerpts and reflective comments by teachers Thelma and Huhana.

Box 6.3

Kayla's story: excerpts from Learning Stories and reflections from Thelma and Huhana, two of her kaiako (teachers)

November. Oral language. We commented that there was a great improvement in her language, its enunciation and articulation. We wondered if the revisiting of the portfolios had enabled this improved language development. It would appear that it enhanced her vocabulary acquisition and the repetitive nature of the revisiting gave her confidence. We wondered whether the revisiting contributed to Kayla's identity, her sense of knowing, being and doing. What part has repetition played? Kayla, of all the children, has been the most frequent visitor, not only of her own but of other children's portfolios and of the wall documentation. Did it confirm her place in our centre community and enable a growing confidence?

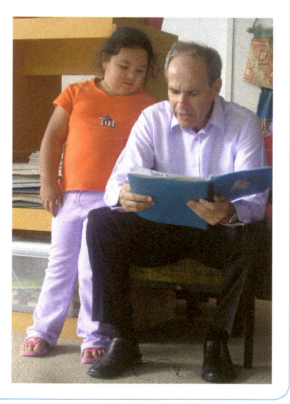

February of the following year. Koru patterns and tā moko. A Learning Story is written about Kayla's first interest in the tā moko, entitled 'Fascination', and in the coming weeks Kayla returns frequently to revisit the photograph in this story.

March. Photographs. The Mayor of the city visited the centre, and Kayla shared her portfolio with him. A photograph was taken and the teachers pinned it up on the wall during the holidays. When she arrived back after the Easter holidays one of the boys called her over to show her the photograph. Thelma later commented that 'this was a very special moment' as the boys did not often interact with Kayla.

April. Drawing and using books for reference. Kayla begins to draw tā moko patterns: 'Whaea![1] Look at my koru.' Huhana (a teacher): 'She wasn't interested in anything with pens, nothing, she would just go and sit in different places in the centre and observe. So this was a real breakthrough. Now she wants pens, but not any pens, it has to be particular pens.' Thelma: 'A red pen for the red design … From there she went on to mask-making because in one of the books there was a carving and it was the same shape as that.'

April and May. Mask-making, painting and clay work. Kayla joins with other children to make masks with tā moko patterns on them, and a collaborative wall painting with a theme of koru patterns. The painting stayed on the wall, and the children added to it from time to time. The koru pattern is used by Kayla in clay work, and in painting with a group of children.

Mid June. Using a book and a jigsaw for reference. Kayla finds a picture of te wharenui in the book with the tā moko pictures. 'Whaea, the marae! We got the puzzle!' exclaimed Kayla. They find the puzzle and she quizzes one of the

teachers about the names of the designs, and repeats them in Māori. Huhana writes a Learning Story (which includes six photographs of the event).

Late June. Patterns in carvings. Another Learning Story is written when the teachers and the children visit a wharenui at a nearby tertiary institute. In a Learning Story Thelma comments: Kayla

(Continued)

(Continued)

was very excited and we wondered if she would make the links to her interest in tā moko and koru designs. Kayla went to explore the carvings and immediately pointed out a koru design to me. 'Look, whaea, a koru.' With a smile on her face she continued to wander around the wharenui looking at the carvings in particular.

Music and rhythm. In a reflection about this story, Thelma adds that Kayla appears to prefer circular designs rather than angular and that koru patterns are more fluid and rhythmic. She wonders whether her developing confidence with te reo Māori (Māori language) at the centre is because it is a musical and rhythmic language and notes that she also enjoys music and singing.

Late June. Literacy. Reflection from Thelma: The koru patterns and spirals have also become Kayla's literacy links. Through them she has developed an interest in letter formation and is beginning to make the initial letters of her name.

She pointed out to me that an 'e' shape looked like a koru, even though she didn't know the name for the letter. As Kayla goes to school I wonder if she will make the connections to literacy through her art. She certainly is already. A Learning Story of this writing is accompanied by five photographs.

July. Collaborative drawing and construction. A story with five photographs is written of Kayla joining together with other children to draw kowhaiwhai patterns on strips of card as part of a collaborative project. Huhana writes the story, and concludes with a reflection: 'I wonder if Kayla's own research has enabled her to break through the uncertainties she once had of herself and her abilities. I noticed she does not have her portfolio nearby, which she often reflected on. Or was the portfolio her only source of knowledge before tā moko?'

[1]Glossary of words in Māori: kowhaiwhai patterns = rafter patterns in a meeting house; tamariki = children; tā moko = tattoo; korero = talk; Whaea = term of respect for the teacher (often loosely translated as 'Auntie'); te wharenui = traditional Māori meeting house.

There are many chains of learning episodes here: the development of her oral language was the chain of greatest interest to her speech language therapist, but other chains were about a growing interest and expertise in koru patterns and tā moko as she made links between a number of sources to point out similarities and differences, her drawings that became more elaborate, her clay work on the same topic and her increasing comfort with collaborative work. It is difficult to disentangle these chains, and it is just this tangle that, over time, describes her growing learner identity.

Relevant to this notion of a 'tangle' is a research project by Chris Lepper, Denise Williamson and Joy Cullen (2003) in which a number of experts met together to review the Learning Story portfolios for two case studies of children with additional learning needs. The specialists, the Education Support Workers and the families each highlighted different 'languages'; the Learning Stories kept the tangle of significant chains together, and researchers wondered whether the Learning Stories could 'speak' to all these experts. They were interested in:

> exploring learning story assessment as a means for promoting a community of practice with all participants in the team working with a child with complex needs, including early childhood teachers, special education staff, hospital therapists, parents and education support workers. (Lepper, Williamson and Cullen, 2003: 20)

One of the parents commented on 'all the different languages' that were used in her child's assessments (p. 20):

> If learning stories had been in place at the start then we wouldn't have been struggling with all the different languages they (professionals) used. With learning stories everyone is on an even playing field.

The authors noted (p. 22) that 'the use of a shared "assessment/planning" tool supported the community of practice concept by encouraging a shared language and climate of support amongst the team'. The speech language therapist was able to code a narrative learning story that she had written from her specialised perspective and said that she had learned about the child's functional language from the everyday settings of the stories. This was a study of limited scope (two children), but it raised interesting questions about the possibilities of more integrated approaches, mediated by Learning Stories, for children with complex additional needs. These opportunities would have to include being able to do some untangling of the different chains of interest, while still keeping the interdisciplinary story available for the child and the family. A Ministry of Education publication has continued these explorations in a book to accompany school narrative assessment exemplars for learners with special education needs (Ministry of Education, 2009b).

Concluding Comments

This chapter has illustrated the way in which Learning Stories can recognise and document the complexity of ways in which learners appropriate knowledges and dispositions, and it has emphasised the ways in which they have responded to the twenty-first century digital revolution. Digital technology has changed the ways in which Learning Stories are written, and changed the ways in which we communicate and 'do literacy'. This chapter has emphasised the distribution of learning across an affordance network of languages and resources, and we can talk about 'distributed cognitions' (Salomon, 1993) or 'distributed intelligence' (Perkins, 1993: 89) in which resources and a repertoire of languages are an integral part of thinking and communicating, reducing the 'cognitive load' for young children of recall and explanation. David Perkins has given the name 'person-plus' to refer to the person plus the resources in his or her surround, and in Chapter 1 we saw that Wertsch spoke of 'individual(s)-acting-with-mediational-means' adding that 'a focus on mediated action and the cultural tools employed in it makes it possible to "live in the middle" and to address the cultural situatedness of action, power and authority' (Wertsch, 1998: 65).

Kayla's story illustrated that her portfolio of Learning Stories was also a mediational means, playing a role in developing her growing expertise and her identity as a learner with expertise valued by her peers. Ann Brown and colleagues wrote about 'distributed expertise' in a classroom in which children select topics of interest and become 'resident experts' (Brown, Ash, Rutherford, Nakagawa, Gordon and Campione, 1993: 202). Kayla's teacher noted that 'other children sought her out for the knowledge and expertise that she was acquiring'.

This chapter is the final in the series of four chapters about the themes and consequences, the opportunities and affordances, of using a narrative format for assessment with the aim of constructing and strengthening learner identities. Chapter 7 will zoom out from episodes and chains of episodes to canvas some ideas about balance and progression.

Note

1 Carlina Rinaldi's writings, speeches and interviews have been gathered together in a 2006 book, *In Dialogue with Reggio Emilia: Listening, Researching and Learning*. There are a number of aspects of the Reggio Emilia theory and practice that resonate with the early childhood Learning Story work in New Zealand, an island bicultural nation in the South Pacific. Here we mention three: the power of documentation; the child as competent and strong; and the interest and excitement of the children as they make meaning in a range of modes – the 'hundred languages of children'. In a chapter on documentation and assessment, Rinaldi (2006) emphasises the

value of documentation 'as a tool for recalling; that is, as a possibility for reflection' (p. 63). She notes that in the Reggio Emilia schools, the documentation (video and audio recordings, written notes) is collected, sometimes catalogued, and brought back for rereading, revisiting and reconstruction of the experience. She adds:

> In fact, I believe that documentation is a substantial part of the goal that has always characterised our experience: the search for meaning – to find the meaning of school, or rather, to construct the meaning of school, as a place that plays an active role in the children's search for meaning and our own search for meaning (and shared meanings).

> The search for the meaning of life and of the self in life is born with the child and is desired by the child. This is why we talk about a child who is competent and strong – a child who has the right to hope and the right to be valued, not a predefined child seen as fragile, needy, incapable. (p. 63, 64)

This chapter was about 'distributed' learning, and in the literature, the 1993 book edited by Gavriel Salomon on *Distributed cognitions: Psychological and educational considerations* has been influential. In more recent times, research on the affordance of information communication technologies has dominated the field, but the Reggio Emilia experience brings us back to some of the other important languages that children in the early years are developing. Often they are 'concrete': construction, drawing, painting and, as Papert says, these modes are lifelong modes for meaning-making, not just for young children. Carolyn Edwards, Lella Gandini and George Forman (1998) have edited a collection on the Reggio Emilia projects called *The hundred languages of children*, the name of an exhibition conceived by Loris Malaguzzi, and emphasising the range of ways in which the children at Reggio make meaning.

7

Reconceptualising Assessment

Box 7.1

We need to make a mind shift in terms of how do we go about assessing key competencies. You can't go and tick off I'm a caring citizen, I participate and contribute, I'm a thinker. That form of assessment doesn't sit comfortably with key competencies 'cos these are attributes, dispositions that we are developing throughout our lives, so as an adult I'm still developing as a thinker. So teachers need to make that shift from the tick box mentality. What's a better way? How can I show development and growth in the key competencies? How am I going to show that children are reflecting on their learning? Learning Stories have the ability to do that in a very powerful way. ... Certainly from my point of view it was very much about leading by example, sharing what I was doing, sharing my enthusiasm and passion for Learning Stories. (Gary, Primary School Principal. In Davis, Carr, Wright and Peters, forthcoming)

Gary is arguing for a reconceptualising of assessment when we want assessment to do some of the work towards constructing a learner identity – as a caring citizen, as a thinker – and to contribute to the strengthening of 'dispositions that we are developing throughout our lives'. Learning Stories are an attempt to capture these aspects of learning, while at the same time providing a site for teachers and learners to co-construct learning journeys and learning pathways. This chapter returns to two categories of learning outcome that have been discussed in this book (the intermingling of stores of knowledge and stores of disposition) and the four themes that have described the consequences of Learning Stories as formative assessment practice. Finally, this chapter suggests that each of these four themes can be seen as a 'balancing act' and as representing a dimension of strengthening or progression. The chapter also sets out four design principles for an assessment practice that has learner identities in mind, and briefly adds a fifth theme or dimension for further thought.

The Intermingling of Stores of Knowledge and Stores of Disposition

Every chapter in this book has highlighted the interdependence of 'content' knowledge (and the development and use of it) and 'dispositional' knowledge (and the development and use of it), introduced in Chapter 1, and Table 4.1 includes eight examples of this interdependence. Kyah's interest in collage and fabric art was combined with her disposition to adapt and improvise with the resources available. Learning Stories documented Diana's growing knowledge about te reo Māori and karate; at the same time her positive educational experience in the repertoire of topic-based workshops that the school provided was supporting her disposition towards 'trying something new'. Zeb was taking on the identity of a scientist. The combination of expertise (knowing about fish, skills of categorisation, information about their behaviour and the scientific language to talk about them) was growing alongside a readiness to refine his habits of attention, explanation, analogy and sensory exploration, together with innovative strategies for measuring using units of measurement ready to hand and for making connections with other contexts. Later, he would call on some of these strategies of meaning-making in another science topic with fewer opportunities for hands-on exploration: volcanoes.

Devya's teachers record his expertise on, and passion for, the topic of temples and gods, including his disposition to represent his ideas in a range of ways. For Rangitahuri, Apirana and the Anuhe group of children, their hands-on knowledge of the garden accompanied their immersion in the cultural ways of knowing being reflected in the philosophy and values at the kōhanga reo. For Emmanuel, the 'boundary-crossing' affordances of particular objects (toy wild animals) enabled his gradual ability and inclination to communicate with others and to participate in a group. Charleeh-Blu's developing skills in drawing and painting later played a part in her disposition for empathy and caring. Kayla's learning journey traces the intertwining of a growing expertise and interest in tā moko with her increasing confidence in social situations; it was her expertise – and the photograph from a Learning Story of her sharing her portfolio with the city Mayor – that opened the door to acceptance by other children. In every case the learning environment and the assessment practice played a key role in this learning.

The book has highlighted some of the ways in which teachers and learners have collected evidence of this learning and then used this evidence to assess and support it. Stories keep faith with the close interconnection of the subject-based with the dispositional. But even primarily subject-based learning is often attached to the affording environment in such complex ways as to warrant 'prose descriptions'. In a discussion of a teacher's practice as she teaches mathematics to a diverse group of fifth graders, Pamela Moss provides an example of a teacher who reports to parents in 'prose descriptions' of the students' mathematical processes. Moss draws on data from a 2001 book written by the teacher, Magdalene Lampert, about her teaching. She (Moss, 2008: 252) makes a comment about how this teacher reports to parents: 'We see, as well, one example of how Lampert reports to parents about their children's progress – prose descriptions of what they have accomplished and what they have to work on – which is intended to represent the complexity of their mathematical performance in ways that grades cannot.'

We have concluded that Learning Stories can capture the intermingling of expertise and disposition, the connections with the local environment that provide cues for further planning, the positioning of the assessment inside a learning journey, and the interdependence of the social, cognitive and affective dimensions of learning experiences. At the same time Learning Stories enable children and students to develop capacities for self-assessment and for reflecting on their learning. They are literally artifacts too (see photo).

Mia had drawn pictures of all the teachers and then used her portfolio as a tool to add their names to her drawing.

The Four Themes

The previous four chapters have described four consequences, and therefore purposes, of a narrative approach to educational assessment. Learning Stories have responded to the demands and challenges of: co-authoring curriculum and assessment and devolving some of the agency for learning to the learner (Chapter 3); connecting with communities outside the classroom and encouraging reciprocal engagement with families (Chapter 4); recognising learning journeys and the continuities of the learning over time (Chapter 5); and appropriating a repertoire of practices where the learning is distributed over a number of languages and other modes of meaning-making (Chapter 6). In an interview for a DVD of Learning Stories in schools (Davis, Carr, Wright and Peters, forthcoming), Gary has talked about the first Learning Story that he wrote, at a professional development workshop. This was a story about cooperation that he had noticed and recognised as a significant episode for nine-year-old Raymond at this point in his learning journey. The story that Gary wrote avoided deficit positioning and placed the story as an event on a learning journey – in this case towards being a caring citizen. It became a public affirmation of a possible self, of great interest to Raymond and his grandmother:

> And so I sat down with Raymond and shared this with him and he took it home, and a couple of days later I ran into the grandmother at school. She actually came up to me and started talking about the Learning Story and how wonderful Raymond thought it was, and how proud of it. She shared with me at the time that it was sitting on their fridge at home. And so from that early moment I thought that Learning Stories had this very powerful ability to engage students in their learning and I thought if I can engage Raymond I'll be able to engage most children. (Interview with Gary in Davis, Carr, Wright and Peters, forthcoming)

Raymond also comments in an interview: 'My Nan was really impressed with that and I haven't quite done that before so she was really impressed with it. I was impressed with myself.' Later, he begins to write his own Learning Stories and says: 'I like them because it can express your feelings.' Three of the themes about the consequences of this assessment practice in this book are in evidence here: agency, connection with family and continuity. And Raymond has alerted us to take note of the affective element in learning, implicit in discussions of dispositions.

Balancing Goals and Interests and Practices

Formative assessments designed to provide feedback to learners and their families will reflect balances that have been struck between discussion and documentation, between participation and reification (Cowie and Carr, 2004: 106), and each of the four themes in this book reflects a balancing act:

- authoring (on one's own) *and* co-authoring in dialogue;

- teaching and assessing inside the classroom *and* engaging families in the process and making the story relevant to the world outside;

- documenting expertise at one moment in time *and* constructing chains of linked episodes, finding planning directions and keeping an eye on learner identities; and

- focusing on one language or mode at a time *and* focusing on an interest or task that requires a multimodal approach.

These balances are summarised in Table 7.1 on p. 136. Individual teachers, learners, families, preschools, schools and governments take privileged positions in these balancing acts and these positions will be aligned with their beliefs about learning, about children, about assessment and about curriculum. These beliefs may not be flexible enough to respond to local situations and individual learners. In team-teaching early childhood centres where teachers do not have the opportunity for regular discussions of the children's Learning Stories, connecting up chains of significance in portfolios  will be difficult. And these balances are always subject to dialogue. The teachers in this book have been engaged in just such dialogue, and we hope that this book will be a further catalyst for teacher discussions.

We take our cue from Robert Sternberg and colleagues (2007), writing about wisdom and education, who suggest that wise teaching and learning includes a balancing of intrapersonal, interpersonal and extrapersonal interests, and a balancing of short- and long-term goals. We have explored these ideas with teachers, and raise them here as topics for further discussion. In his 2002 book *Making Stories: Law, Literature and Life*, Jerome Bruner sets out the balancing act in this self-making work. Referring to autobiography, he says:

> A self-making narrative is something of a balancing act. It must, on the one hand, create a conviction of autonomy, that one has a will of one's own, a certain freedom of choice, a degree of possibility. But it must also relate the self to a world of others – to friends and family, to institutions, to the past, to reference groups. But the commitment to others that is implicit in relating oneself to others of course limits our autonomy. We seem unable to live without both, autonomy and commitment, and our lives strive to balance the two. So do the self-narratives we tell ourselves. (p. 78)

So too does a portfolio of Learning Stories strive to balance autonomy and commitment to a world of others: to balance the goals and interests of agency, interpersonal dialogue and the wider community. These considerations challenge any assessment practice. A *test* provides an individual measure at one particular time, while a *story* of the target skill or knowledge or disposition, in the process of developing, can include the interpersonal and the wider community and the opportunities that they have provided, and could provide. Robyn G. commented on the idea that Emmanuel was finding a balance between making meaning on his own, with his toy animals, and participating in the group:

> Emmanuel has been doing lots more things since July. I made a reference here that he [now] knows these children very well and that they share a language, in a way, of life in the past. I've been reading Vivien Gussin Paley's *White Teacher* and in that she suggests that children have more in common with one another than they do with their teachers and that play is the original open-ended and integrated curriculum. I like that very much. Children don't ask other children 'where did you come from?' they ask 'what role will you play?' So he joined in all the singing and his fingers can't resist the beat of the music so he had his drum with him and sang and enjoyed that. I thought, well, I recognised that he found a place of balance. He has spent many hours absorbed with his animals with small interactions with other children and some movement towards other interests. So today I noticed that balance of watching and active participation and I think we can see that here. (Robyn, reflections on a video of Emmanuel at play, aged three-and-a half)

These balances are being achieved inside the local learning environment; it can be an additional challenge to achieve some balance between inside and outside the early childhood centre or classroom. Etienne Wenger (1998) comments:

> I have argued that an educational design does not enable learning by attempting to substitute for the world and be the entire learning event. It cannot be a closed system that shelters a well-engineered but self-contained learning process. On the contrary, it must aim to offer dense connections to communities outside the setting. (p. 275)

Lorraine, in an interview during the question-asking and question-exploring research project commented on the building of the centre's new playground and their interest in ensuring that children had the opportunity to, at least, observe 'Real Work':

> We wouldn't have done this (build the playground during a weekday) two years ago: we would have left what was outside the gate outside the gate. Now we are bringing that inside and we are going out more. So the playground would be an example of that. In the past we would have had that playground sorted in the weekend! ... We quickly learnt how to read the tape 'Warning, Danger, Keep Out' and the children watched their (the playground construction workers') designs, their intentions, unfold over days or weeks as experts worked to build stone walls for the garden, our stone water feature and the like. Much later, as we reflected on our children's deep, deep involvement in these experiences, we realised that 'our teaching was different from before'. (Malaguzzi, 1993: 77) (Lorraine, writing in Greerton Early Childhood Centre Team et al., 2008)

No one side of the balance is always the right one; it will depend on the circumstance. It is, however, worthwhile considering these balances in our centres and classrooms, and to ask whether the balance always sits in one place, and whether alternatives might reflect the innovative and thoughtful *adaptive expertise* that young people will need, as well as the efficient domain-specific skills, to cope with a complex world and open-ended problems.

Furthermore, there is inevitably a central balance, or negotiated trade-off, that encapsulates much of any assessment discussion. Moss, Girard and Greeno (2008: 300) write about 'endogenous assessment', based on shared and evolving experience, and 'exogenous assessment' where judgements of expertise are based on externally relevant standards. They quote Jordan and Putz (2004: 356) who say that 'the question that remains to be answered is, how we negotiate the trade-off between the requirements of institutions that need comparable numbers and objective measurements for their purposes and the learners and teachers in classrooms and workplaces who need endogenous assessment derived from the activity to be mastered?'

> Awareness of complementary assessment methods and their specific affordances, drawbacks, and unintended consequences could be a step toward collaborative code-sign of new organizational structures within which endogenous as well as exogenous, informal as well as formal, evaluation criteria can flourish. (Jordan and Putz, 2004: 356 in Moss, Girard and Greeno, 2008: 300)

Dimensions of Strength or Progression

One of these balances is to do with short, middle-level and longer-term time frames. Learning can be analysed as short chains of episodes, as we have discussed in Chapter 5 and, using Kayla's example of her progression along a number of languages and modes, Chapter 6. The discussion of this balancing act follows on from Jay Lemke's critical comment in Chapter 5: 'We can see the short-term development of a meaningful practice, but not the longer term development of a meaning-making disposition, an attitudinal stance, a habitus.' There is a sense in which the four themes in this book provide some broad and more general guidelines as longer term dimensions of strength, dimensions that are just as entangled together as Kayla's modes of meaning-making (see Table 7.1). During the *Key Learning Competencies Across Place and Time* research project, together with the project that led to *Kei Tua o te Pae*, four 'dimensions of strength' were developed (Carr, Lee and Jones, 2007).

These four dimensions are a way of describing a multi-path learning trajectory. They have been dubbed the 'ABCD' dimensions, and they parallel the themes in this book. If we take Diana's learning journey as an example, we can say that the key competency 'participating and contributing' was being strengthened along these four dimensions, and that this worked to sustain her learning identity as someone with the courage to 'try something new'. The school and the teachers, Nikki and Susie, co-constructed with Diana and her mother both the pathway (the opportunities to learn) and the journey that Diana actually took. The journey began when the teachers brainstormed ideas about the key competencies with the children.

Table 7.1   Purposes and consequences, balancing acts and dimensions of progress

	Agency	Breadth	Continuities	Distribution
Purposes for and consequences of Learning Stories for children and families	Co-authoring curriculum and assessment (Chapter 3)	Connecting with communities outside the classroom and encouraging reciprocal engagement with families (Chapter 4)	Recognising learning journeys and the continuities of the learning over time (Chapter 5)	Distributing the learning across languages and modes: appropriating a repertoire of practices where the learning is distributed over a number of languages and other modes of meaning-making (Chapter 6)
Balancing goals and interests	Working things out for oneself *and* engaging in dialogue	Local classroom and early childhood centre focus *and* communicating with family and keeping the learning relevant to the wider community	Documenting expertise at one moment in time *and* constructing chains of linked episodes, finding planning directions *and* keeping an eye on developing longer-term learner identities	A focus on one language or mode at a time *and* a focus on an interest or open-ended task that may require a multimodal approach
Dimensions of progress	Children initiate their own learning pathways and journeys and are becoming self-assessors. They can dialogue about their learning with increasing confidence and competence	Stronger and more diverse connections are made with family and community knowledges and interests, outside the centre and the classroom	Chains of learning episodes are recognised and negotiated, linking the present with the past and the future. The 'next steps' are more frequently co-constructed. So are longer term visions and possible selves	The learning is distributed across an increasing number of languages and modes of representing and communicating and they may be combined in increasingly complex ways

Agency: Diana was one of the children consulted about the meaning of this key competency, and, having personalised these ideas in her own words as 'trying something new', she had the option of choosing a range of interesting and challenging workshops. A group dance task provided the opportunity for the children to develop a dance piece together, and for Diana to take the lead at one point.

Breadth: There was a 'repertoire of places' established in which she could try something new and the Learning Stories went home with her mother (who was welcome at the school, and also wrote a Learning Story for Diana's portfolio). Diana's mother, too, decided to try something that she had not done before (having her face painted when she went as a parent help to the school camp).

Continuity: Diana was, together with the teachers, her mother and her peers, co-constructing a pathway that made sense to her. The local 'scripts' available were of assistance in this process. She was invited to practise being courageous in situations like the karate workshop where she was a 'little scared', and the sequence of episodes was documented by Nikki and Susie, including a commentary on the learning. That documentation was available for revisiting and conversations about progress and ideas for 'What next'.

Distribution: As part of the brainstorm exercises on 'participation', all the class tried new activities. Diana then went on to participate in activities under the umbrella goal of 'trying something new' that engaged different modes: gesture and music (a dance workshop and later the karate workshop), singing and oral language (the te reo workshop). Table 7.1 sets out these four dimensions of strength, aligned with the themes in this book.

Four Assessment Design Principles

The writing of this book has led us to four design principles for assessment practices, and has interrogated Learning Stories for their capacity to turn these principles into action. Assessment practices will:

Position learners with agency. In co-authoring and co-constructing practices they will provide a context for dialogue, in order for learners to know what the 'game' is here and to enable them to develop self-assessment capacities and dispositions.

Include multiple voices, and connect with families, other communities and real-world problems they will in order for learners to develop alignments of understanding, expectation and opportunity across places and communities. They will provide a repertoire of aligned but different cultural practices that encourage the capacity for recontextualising learning and a deepening of understanding.

Provide navigation markers for students, markers of the journeys so far and a glimpse of the possible pathway forward. They will therefore enable learners to recognise at least some of the features of the learning journey, their achievements in the past and a vision for the future, for themselves and for the world, and for themselves in the world.

Integrate dispositional knowledge and practice with subject knowledge and practice in a range of modes and with a range of people, resources and activities. An affective element to learning will be acknowledged and sustained. A repertoire of meaning-making practices and 'adaptive expertise' – available when the situation changes – in a number of cultural, material, subject, modal or conceptual spaces will be recognised and supported.

Adding an E

It is our view now that the ABCD dimensions may have downplayed one of the important contributions that Learning Stories can make towards the construction of learner identities. Learning Stories insist on including the dispositional, and they resist deficit positioning. This does not mean that they omit guidance for improvement and further achievement. But they often document, and work to sustain, what has been called the 'passion' for learning in at least one cultural, material, subject, modal or conceptual space. Teachers in this book have written about the children's courage, determination and perseverance, and in a book entitled *Finding flow* (1997), Mihaly Csikszentmihalyi has written about the affective nature of the experience of 'flow', when someone or a group of people, are fully engaged and focused and when their skills are 'fully involved in overcoming a challenge that is just about manageable' (p. 30). Flow occurs when goals are clear, feedback is relevant and challenges and skills are in balance (p. 31).

Perhaps Learning Stories, in part, work towards emphasising and constructing those chains of 'flow' episodes that are so important for our well-being, that make for 'excellence in life' as Csikszentmihalyi puts it (1997: 32). Carol Dweck has noted their importance when she writes about feedback (in Chapter 1); Diana was pushing herself into positions of potential flow when she was trying something new (in Chapter 2); and Raymond emphasised this point when he articulated that he liked writing his own Learning Stories because he could include his feelings. Csikszentmihalyi's (1997: 33) research indicates that 'the flow experience acts as a magnet for learning – that is, for developing new levels of challenges and skills', and in his earlier book on creativity (1996) he noted the importance of intense interest and curiosity in the early years. These are qualities of affect, and have been illustrated in many of the stories in this book.

A comment about this excitement, and a photograph (see opposite), comes from a parent whose third child, Tessa, had just begun attending 'Emmett St', an early childhood centre. Jo, the parent, writes the following for Tessa's folder of Learning Stories:

> It was an exciting day in the Harvey household when Tessa started at Emmett St., and a rite of passage when her folder came home for the first time. This prompted Amelia to bring hers home too. As soon as I arrived to pick her (Amelia) up, off she went to grab her folder. Not to be outdone, Ezra dug his out of storage and so the story swapping began!!

This emphasis on affect includes the sustaining of a *teacher's* enthusiasm for teaching as well. Gary, at the start of this chapter, uses the words 'enthusiasm' and 'passion' about his assessment practice. It is this quality that enables us to argue that Learning Stories construct student *and teacher* identities. So when we have talked about the ABCD of dimensions of strength to teachers, they have, on more than one occasion, argued for an E. E for Excitement, Enthusiasm, Exuberance and Élan (the notion of 'élan' is rather nice here, with our interest in 'trajectories' of learning, since our Collins dictionary says that it comes from the French *élancer*, to *throw forth*, ultimately from the Latin *lancea*, a lance). Na'ilah

Suad Nasir, Ann Rosebery, Beth Warren and Carol Lee (2006: 489, 499), writing about 'youths from nondominant groups' argued that 'designing learning environments for these students must address the multiple (and often neglected) elements of learning, including identity and affect'. Teachers have often transmitted in the Learning Stories their own sense of excitement and enthusiasm about the learning that they describe, an enthusiasm that is contagious for both families and children, influencing aspirations and perspectives on possible selves. This affective dimension can thus be added as a consequence of a Learning Story construction or co-construction – and the revisiting of a Learning Story in the early childhood centre, school classroom or at home. Raymond and his grandmother called this 'being proud', and 'being impressed', affective consequences of great significance for the construction of learner identities.

References

Absolum, M., Flockton, L., Hattie, J., Hipkins, R. and Reid, L. (2009). *Directions for assessment in New Zealand* (DANZ). Wellington: Ministry of Education.

Barab, S., Hay, K. and Yamagata-Lynch, L. (2001). Constructing networks of action-relevant episodes: An in situ research methodology. *Journal of the Learning Sciences*, 10(1/2), 63–112.

Barron, B. (2006). Interest and self-sustained learning as catalysts of development: A learning ecology perspective. *Human Development*, 49, 193–224.

Bird, A. and Reese, E. (2006). Emotional reminiscing and the development of an autobiographical self. *Developmental Psychology*, 42(4), 613–26.

Black, P. and Wiliam, D. (1998a). Assessment and classroom learning. *Assessment in Education: Principles, Policy & Practice*, 5(1), 7–74.

Black, P. and Wiliam, D. (1998b). *Inside the black box: Raising standards through classroom assessment*. London: King's College London, School of Education.

Black, P., Harrison, C., Lee, C., Marshall, B. and Wiliam, D. (2002). *Working inside the black box: Assessment for learning in the classroom*. London: NferNelson.

Black, P., Harrison, C., Lee, C., Marshall, B. and Wiliam, D. (2003). *Assessment for learning: putting it into practice*. Maidenhead: Open University Press.

Black, P., McCormick, R., James, M. and Pedder, D. (2006). Learning how to learn and assessment for learning: A theoretical inquiry. *Research Papers in Education*, 21(2), 119–32.

Bourdieu, P. (1990). *The logic of practice*, trans. R. Nice. Cambridge: Polity.

Braidotti, R. (1994). *Nomadic subjects: Embodiment and sexual difference in contemporary feminist theory*. New York: Columbia University Press.

Bransford, J.D., Barron, B., Pea, R.D., Metzolt, A., Kuhl, P., Bell, P., Stevens. R. et al. (2006). Foundations and opportunities for an interdisciplinary science of learning. In R.K. Sawyer (ed.), *The Cambridge handbook of the learning sciences*. New York: Cambridge University Press, 19–34.

Bronfenbrenner, U. (1979). *Ecology of human development*. Cambridge, MA: Harvard University Press.

Brooker, L. (2002). *Starting school: Young children learning cultures*. Buckingham: Open University Press.

Brown, A.L., Ash, D., Rutherford, M., Nakagawa, K., Gordon, A. and Campione, J.C. (1993). Distributed expertise in the classroom. In G. Salomon (ed.) *Distributed cognitions: Psychological and educational considerations*. Cambridge: Cambridge University Press, 188–228.

Bruner, J. (2002). *Making stories: Law, literature, life*. Cambridge, MA: Harvard University Press.

Burke, K. (1945). *A grammar of motives*. New York: Prentice Hall.

Buxton, J. (2002). *Keep trying*. Wellington: Learning Media.

Carr, M. (1998). *Assessing children's learning in early childhood settings: A professional development programme for discussion and reflection – support booklet and videos: What to assess, why assess, how to assess?* Wellington: NZCER Press.

Carr, M. (2000). Seeking children's perspectives about their learning. In A.B. Smith, N.J. Taylor and M.M. Gollop (eds), *Children's voices: Research, policy and practice*. Auckland: Pearson, 37–55.

Carr, M. (2001a). *Assessment in early childhood settings: Learning stories.* London: Paul Chapman.

Carr, M. (2001b). A sociocultural approach to learning orientation in an early childhood setting. *Qualitative Studies in Education,* 14(4), 525–42.

Carr, M. (2005). The leading edge of learning: recognising children's success as learners. *European Journal of Early Childhood Research,* 13(2), 41–50.

Carr, M. (2008). Can assessment unlock and open the doors to resourcefulness and agency? In S. Swaffield (ed.), *Unlocking Assessment.* London: Routledge, 36–54.

Carr, M. (2009). Kei tua o te pae: Assessing learning that reaches beyond the self and beyond the horizon. *Assessment Matters,* 1, 20–47.

Carr, M. (forthcoming). Young children reflecting on their learning: Teachers' conversation strategies. *International Journal of Early Years.*

Carr, M., Hatherly, A., Lee, W. and Ramsey, K. (2003). Te Whāriki and assessment: a case study of teacher change. In J. Nuttall (ed.) *Weaving Te Whāriki. Aotearoa's early childhood curriculam document in theory and practice.* Wellington, NZ: NZCER Press, 188–214.

Carr, M., Jones, C. and Lee, W. (2010). Learning journeys. In W. Drewery and L. Claiborne (eds), *Human development: family, place, culture.* Sydney: McGraw-Hill.

Carr, M., Lee, W. and Jones, C. (2004, 2007, 2009). *Kei tua o te pae: Assessment for learning: Early childhood exemplars.* Books 1–20. A resource prepared for the Ministry of Education. Wellington: Learning Media.

Carr, M., Peters, S., Davis, K., Bartlett, C., Bashford, N., Berry, P., Greenslade, S., Molloy, S., O'Connor, N., Simpson, M., Smith, Y., Williams, T. and Wilson-Tukaki, A. (2008). *Key learning competencies across place and time: Kimihia te ara totika, hei oranga mo to ao.* Final report to the Ministry of Education. Wellington, NZ: NZCER.

Carr, M., Smith, A.B., Duncan, J., Jones, C., Lee, W. and Marshall, K. (2010). *Learning in the making.* Rotterdam: Sense.

Clandinin, D.J. (ed.) (2007). *Handbook of narrative inquiry: Mapping a methodology.* Thousand Oaks, CA: Sage.

Clarkin-Phillips, J. and Carr, M. (forthcoming). An affordance network for engagement: Increasing parent and family agency in an early childhood education setting. *European Early Childhood Education Research Journal.*

Claxton, G. (2004). Learning is learnable (and we ought to teach it). In S.J. Cassell (ed.), *Ten years on report.* Bristol: National Commission for Education.

Claxton, G. (2009). Forward. In R. Delany, L. Day and M. R. Chambers (eds), *Learning power heroes.* Bristol: TLO Ltd.

Claxton, G., Chambers, M., Powell, G. and Lucas, B. (2011). *The learning powered school: A blueprint for 21st century education.* Bristol: TLO Ltd.

Cochran-Smith, M. and Donnell, K. (2006). Practitioner inquiry: Blurring the boundaries of research and practice. In J.L. Green, G. Camilli, P.B. Elmore, A. Skukaus Kaité and P. Grace (eds), *Handbook of complementary methods in education research.* Washington, DC: AERA; and Mahwah, NJ: Erlbaum.

Colbert, J. (2006) New forms of an old art – children's storytelling and ICT. *Early Childhood Folio,* 10, 2–5.

Commonwealth of Australia (2009). *Belonging, being, becoming.* Canberra: Australian Government Department of Education, Employment and Workplace Relations for the Council of Australian Governments.

Cowie, B. (2000). Formative assessment in science classrooms. PhD thesis, University of Waikato, Hamilton.

Cowie, B. and Carr, M. (2004). The consequences of socio-cultural assessment. In A. Anning, J. Cullen and M. Fleer (eds), *Early childhood education: Society and culture* (2nd edn, 2009). London: Sage, 95–106.

Crowley, K. and Jacobs, M. (2002). Building islands of expertise in everyday family life. In G. Leinhardt, K. Crowley and K. Knutson (eds), *Learning conversations in museums*. Mahwah, NJ: Lawrence Erlbaum, 333–56.

Csikszentmihalyi, M. (1996). *Creativity: Flow and the psychology of discovery and invention*, 1st edn. New York: Harper Collins.

Csikszentmihalyi, M. (1997) *Finding flow: The psychology of engagement with everyday life*. New York: Harper Collins.

Dahlberg, G. and Moss, P. (2005). *Ethics and politics in early childhood education*. London: Roultedge Falmer.

Davis, K., Carr, M., Wright, J. and Peters, S. (forthcoming). *Monitoring and encouraging the key competencies: Learning stories. Dialogue, connections and plain language reporting*. Wellington, NZ: NZCER Press.

Dweck, C. (1986). Motivational processes affecting learning. *American Psychologist*, 41(10), 1040–8.

Dweck, C. (2000). *Self-theories: Their role in motivation, personality, and development*. Philadelphia, PA: Psychology Press.

Dweck, C. (2006). *Mindset: The new psychology of success*, 1st edn. New York: Random House.

Eberbach, C. and Crowley, K. (2009). From everyday to scientific observation: How children learn to observe the biologist's world. *Review of Educational Research*, 79(1), 39–68.

Ecclestone, K. and Pryor, J. (2003). 'Learning careers' or 'Assessment careers'? The impact of assessment systems on learning. *British Educational Research Journal*, 29(4), 471–88.

Edelstein, W. (2011). Education for democracy: reasons and strategies. *European Journal of Education*, 46(1), part II, 127–37.

Edwards, C., Gandini, L. and Forman, G. (eds) (1998). *The hundred languages of children: The Reggio Emilia Approach – advanced reflections*. Westport, CT: Ablex.

Eisner, E.W. (2005). *Reimagining schools: the selected works of Elliot Eisner*. Abingdon, Oxon: Routledge.

Engestrom, Y., Engestrom, R. and Suntio, A. (2002). Can a school community learn to master it's own future? An activity-theoretical study of expansive learning among middle school teachers. In G. Wells and G. Claxton (eds), *Learning for life in the 21st century: Sociocultural perspectives of the future*. Oxford: Wiley-Blackwell, 211–24.

Filer, A. and Pollard, A. (2000). *The social world of pupil assessment: Processes and contexts of primary schooling*. London: Continuum.

Gee, J.P. (1997). Thinking learning and reading: the situated sociocultural mind. In D. Kirschner and J.A. Whitson (eds), *Situated congition: Semiotic and psychological perspectives*. Chapter 9, 235–259. Mahwah, NJ: Erlbaum.

Gee, J.P. (2000–2001). Identity as an analytic lens for research in education. *Review of Research in Education*, 25, 99–125.

Gee, J.P. (2008). A sociocultural perspective on opportunity to learn. In P.A. Moss, D.C. Pullin, J.P. Gee, L.J. Young and E.H Haerte (eds), *Assessment, equity, and opportunity to learn*. New York: Cambridge University Press.

Gibson, J.J. (1997). The theory of affordances. In R. Shaw and J. Brandsford (eds), *Perceiving, acting and knowing: Toward an ecological psychology*. Hillsdale, MJ: Lawrence Eribaum, 67–82.

Gipps, C. (2002). Sociocultural perspectives on assessment. In G. Wells and G. Claxton (eds), *Learning for life in the 21st century: Sociocultural perspectives on the future of education*. Oxford: Blackwell Publishers, 73–83.

Giudici, C., Rinaldi, C. and Krechevsky, M. (eds) (2001). *Making learning visible: Children as individual and group learners*. Cambridge, MA and Reggio Emilia: Project Zero, Harvard Graduate School of Education and Reggio Children International Center for the Defense and Promotion of the Rights and Potential of all Children.

Gonzàlez, N., Moll, L.C. and Amanti, C. (2005). *Funds of knowledge: Theorizing practice in households, communities, and classrooms*. Mahwah, NJ: L. Erlbaum As sociates.

Greeno, J.G. (2006). Authoritative, accountable positioning and connected, general knowing: Progressive themes in understanding transfer. *Journal of the Learning Sciences*, 15(4), 537–47.

Greeno, J.G. and Gresalfi, M.S. (2008). Opportunities to learn in practice and identity. In P.A. Moss, D.C. Pullin, J.P. Gee, E.H. Haertal and L.J. Young (eds), *Assessment, equity, and opportunity to learn*. New York: Cambridge University Press.

Greenwood, D. and Levin, M. (2008). Reform of the social sciences and of universities through action research. In N. Denzin and Y.S. Lincoln (eds), *The landscape of qualitative research*, 3rd edn. Los Angeles, CA: Sage, 57–86.

Greerton Early Childhood Centre Team, Carr, M. and Lee, W. (2008). *A question-asking and question-exploring culture. Centre of Innovation Final Research Report to the Ministry of Education*. Wellington, NZ: NZCER Press.

Gresalfi, M.S. (2009). Taking up opportunities to learn: Constructing dispositions in mathematics classrooms. *Journal of the Learning Sciences*, 18, 327–69.

Hargreaves, A. and Moore, S. (2000). Educational outcomes, modern and postmodern interpretations: Response to Smyth and Dow. *British Journal of Sociology of Education*, 21(1), 27–42.

Hartley, C., Rogers, P., Smith, J., Peter, S. and Carr, M. (forthcoming). *Across the border: A community negotiates the transition from early childhood to primary school*. Wellington, NZCER Press.

Hattie, J. (2009). *Visible learning: A synthesis of over 800 meta-analyses relating to achievement*. London: Routledge.

Hendry, P.M. (2007) The future of narrative. *Qualitative Inquiry*, 13, 487–98.

Hidi, S., Renninger, K.A. and Krapp, A. (1992). The present state of interest research. In S. Hidi, K.A. Renninger and A. Krapp (eds), *The role of interest in learning and development*. Hillsdale, NJ: Lawrence Erlbaum.

Hipkins, R. (2009). Determining meaning for key competencies via assessment practices. *Assessment Matters*, 1, 4–19.

Holland, D., Lachicotte, W., Skinner, D. and Cain, R. (1998). *Identity and agency in cultural worlds*. Cambridge, Mass.: Harvard University Press.

Hull, G.A. and Katz, M.-L. (2006). Crafting an agentive self: Case studies of digital storytelling. *Research in the Teaching of English*, 41(1), 43–81.

Hutchins, E. (1996). *Cognition in the wild*. Cambridge, MA: MIT Press.

Jewitt, C. (2008). *Technology, literacy, learning: A multimodality approach*. London: Routledge.

Johnston, P. (2004). *Choice words: How our language affects children's learning*. Portland, ME: Stenhouse Publishers.

Jordon, B. and Putz, P. (2004). Assessment as practice: Notes on measures, tests, and targets. *Human Organization, 63*, 346–58.

Kress, G. (2003). *Literacy in the new media age*. London: Routledge.

Lampert, M. (2001). *Teaching problems and problems of teaching*. New Haven, CT: Yale University Press.

Lee, W., Hatherly, A. and Ramsey, K. (2002). Using ICT to document children's learning. *Early Childhood Folio, 6*, 10–16.

Lemke, J.L. (2000). Across the scales of time: Artifacts, activities and meanings in ecosocial systems. *Mind, Culture, and Activity, 7*(4), 273–90.

Lemke, J.L. (2001). The long and the short of it: Comments on multiple timescale studies of human activity. *Journal of the Learning Sciences, 10*(1), 17–26.

Lepper, C., Williamson, D. and Cullen, J. (2003). Professional development to support collaborative assessment. *Early Education, 33*, 19–28.

McNaughton, S. (2002). *Meeting of the minds*. Wellington: Learning Media.

Malaguzzi, L. (1993). History, ideas and basic philosophy. In C. Edwards, L. Gandini and G. Forman (eds), *The hundred languages of children: The Reggio Emilia approach to early childhood education*. Norwood, NJ: Albex, 41–88.

Markus, H. and Nurius, P. (1986). Possible selves. *American Psychologist, 41*(9), 954–69.

Mason, J. (2002). *Researching your own practice: The discipline of noticing*. London: Routledge Falmer.

Meade, A. (ed.) (2005). *Catching the waves: Innovation in early childhood education*. Wellington: NZCER Press.

Meade, A. (ed.) (2006). *Riding the waves: Innovation in early childhood education*. Wellington: NZCER Press.

Meade, A. (ed.) (2007). *Cresting the waves: Innovation in early childhood education*. Wellington: NZCER Press.

Meade, A. (ed.) (2010). *Dispersing waves: Innovation in early childhood education*. Wellington: NZCER Press.

Mercer, N. (2002). Developing dialogues. In G. Wells and G. Claxton (eds), *Learning for life in the 21st century: Sociocultural perspectives on the future of education*. Oxford: Blackwell.

Mercer, N. (2008). The seeds of time: Why classroom dialogue needs a temporal analysis. *Journal of the Learning Sciences, 17*, 33–59.

Mercer, N. and Littleton, K. (2007). *Dialogue and the development of children's thinking: A sociocultural approach*. London: Routledge.

Miller, L. and Pound, L. (eds) (2011). *Theories and approaches to learning in the early years*. London: Sage.

Miller, P. and Goodnow, J. (1995). Cultural practices: Toward an integration of culture and development. In J. Goodnow, P. Miller and F. Kessel (eds), *Cultural practices as contexts for development*. San Francisco, CA: Jossey-Bass. 5–17.

Ministry of Education (1996). *Te whāriki. He whāriki mātauranga mō ngā mokopuna o aotearoa. Early childhood curriculum*. Wellington: Learning Media.

Ministry of Education (2007). *The New Zealand curriculum for English-medium teaching and learning in years 1–13*. Wellington: Learning Media.

Ministry of Education (2009a). *Te whatu pōkeka. Kaupapa maori assessment for learning: Early childhood exemplars*. Wellington: Learning Media.

Ministry of Education (2009b). *Narrative assessment: A guide for teachers. A resource to support the New Zealand Curriculum. Exemplars for learners with special education needs*. Wellington: Learning Media.

Moll, L. C., Amanti, C., Neff, D. and González, N. (1992). Funds of knowledge for teaching: Using a qualitative approach to connect homes and classrooms. *Theory into Practice*, 31(2), 132–41.

Moss, P.A. (2008). Sociocultural implications for assessment I: Classroom assessment. In P.A. Moss, D.C. Pullin, J.P. Gee, E.H Haertel and L.J. Young (eds), *Assessment, equity, and opportunity to learn*. New York: Cambridge University Press, 222–58.

Moss, P.A., Girard, B.J. and Greeno, J.G. (2008). Sociocultural implications for assessment II: Professional learning, evaluation, and accountability. In P.A. Moss, D.C. Pullin, J.P. Gee, E.H. Haertel and L.J. Young (eds), *Assessment, equity, and opportunity to learn*. Cambridge: Cambridge University Press, 295–332.

Moss, P.A., Pullin, D.C., Gee, J.P., Haertel, E.H. and Young, L.J. (eds) (2008). *Assessment, equity, and opportunity to learn*. Cambridge: Cambridge University Press.

Nasir, N.S., Rosebery, A.S., Warren, B. and Lee, C.D. (2006). Learning as a cultural process: Achieving equity through diversity. In R.K. Sawyer (ed.), *The Cambridge handbook of the learning sciences*. New York: Cambridge University Press, 489–504.

Nelson, K. (2000). Narrative, time and the emergence of the encultured self. *Culture & Psychology*, 6(2), 183–96.

Norman, D.A. (1988). *The design of everyday things*. New York: Basic Books.

Nuttall, J. (2003). *Weaving te whāriki: Aotearoa's early childhood curriculum document in theory and practice*. Wellington, NZ: NZCER Press.

Packer, M. and Greco-Brooks, D. (1999). School as a site for the production of persons. *Journal of Constructivist Psychology*, 12, 133–49.

Paley, V. (2004). *A child's work: The importance of fantasy play*. Chicago, IL: University of Chicago Press.

Papert, S. (1980). *Mindstorms*. Brighton: Harvester Wheatsheaf.

Papert, S. (1993). *The children's machine: Rethinking school in the age of the computer*. Hemel Hempstead: Harvester Wheatsheaf.

Perkins, D.N. (1993). Person-plus: A distributed view of thinking and learning. In G. Salomon (ed.), *Distributed cognitions: Psychological and educational considerations*. New York: Cambridge University Press, 111–38.

Perkins, D. (2000). Schools need to pay more attention to 'intelligence in the wild'. *Harvard Education Newsletter*, May/June, 1–3.

Perkins, D.N., Jay, E. and Tishman, S. (1993). Beyond abilities: A dispositional theory of thinking. *Merrill-Palmer Quarterly*, 39(1), 1–21.

Perkins, D., Tishman, S., Ritchhart, R., Donis, K. and Andrade, A. (2000). Intelligence in the wild: A dispositional view of intellectual traits. *Educational Psychology Review*, 12(3), 269–93.

Perry, B., Dockett, S. and Harley, E. (2007). Learning stories and children's powerful mathematics. *Early Childhood Research & Practice*, 9(2).

Pinnegar, S. and Daynes, J.G. (2007). Locating narrative inquiry historically: Thematics in the turn to narrative. In D.J. Clandinin (ed.), *Handbook of narrative inquiry: Mapping a methodology*. Thousand Oaks, CA: Sage Publications.

Pollard, A. and Filer, A. (1999). *The social world of pupil career: Strategic biographies through primary school*. London: Cassell.

Pryor, J. and Crossouard, B. (2008). A socio-cultural theorisation of formative assessment. *Oxford Review of Education*, 34(1), 1–20.

Ramsey, K., Breen, J., Sturm, J., Lee, W. and Carr, M. (2006). *Integrating ICTs with teaching and learning in a New Zealand Kindergarten*. Centre of Innovation Final Research Report to the Ministry of Edukation. Wellingtorr, NZ: Ministry of Education.

Reedy, T. (2003). Toku rangatiratanga na te mana metauranga: Knowledge and power set me free. In J. Nuttall (ed.), *Weaving Te Whariki: Aotearoa New Zealand's document in theory and practice*. Wellington: New Zealand Council for Educational Research.

Reese, E., Suggate, S., Long, J. and Schaughency, E. (2010). Children's oral narrative and reading skills in the first three years of reading instruction. *Reading and Writing*, 23(6), 627–44.

Reissman, C.K. (2008). *Narrative methods for the human sciences*. London: Sage.

Resnick, L. (1987). *Education and learning to think*. Washington, DC: National Academy Press.

Rice, T. (2010). 'The hallmark of a doctor': The stethoscope and the making of medical identity. *Journal of Material Culture*, 15(3), 287–301.

Rinaldi, C. (2006). *In dialogue with Reggio Emilia: Listening, researching, and learning*. London and New York: Routledge.

Ritchhart, R. (2002). *Intellectual character: What it is, why it matters, and how to get it*. San Francisco, CA: Jossey-Bass.

Roth, F., Speece, D. and Cooper, D. (2002). A longitudinal analysis of the connection between oral language and early reading. *Journal of Educational Research*, 95, 259–73.

Rychen, D.S. and Salganik, L.H. (eds) (2001). *Defining and selecting key competencies*. Göttingen: Hogrefe & Huber.

Rychen, D.S. and Salganik, L. H. (eds) (2003*). Key competencies for a successful life and a well-functioning society*. Göttingen: Hogrefe & Huber.

Salomon, G. (ed.) (1993). *Distributed cognitions: Psychological and educational considerations*. New York: Cambridge University Press.

Sfard, A. (2008). *Thinking and communicating: Human development, the growth of discourse, and mathematizing*. Cambridge, UK: Cambridge University Press.

Sfard, A. and Prusak, A. (2005). Telling identities: In search of an analytical tool for investigating learning as a cultural activity. *Educational Researcher*, 34(4), 14–22.

Siraj-Blatchford, I. (2010). A focus on pedagogy: Case studies of effective practice. In K. Sylva, E. Melhuish, P. Sammons, I. Siraj–Blatchford and B. Taggart (eds) *Early childhood matters: Evidence from the effective pre-school and primary education project*. London: Routledge, 149–65.

Smith, A.B. (2011). Relationships with people, places and things: Te Whāriki. In L. Miller and L. Pound (eds), *Theories and approaches to learning in the early years*. London: Sage, 149–62.

Soutar, B. with Te Whānau o Mana Tamariki (2010). Growing raukura. In A. Meade (ed.), *Dispersing waves: Innovation in early childhood education*. Wellington: NZCER Press, 35–40.

Star, S.L. and Griesemer, J.R. (1989). Institutional ecology, 'translations' and boundary objects: Amateurs and professionals in Berkeley's museum of vertebrate zoology, 1907–39. *Social Studies of Science*, 19(3), 387–420.

Sternberg, R.J., Reznitskaya, A. and Janvin, L. (2007). Teaching for wisdom: What matters is not just what students know, but how they use it. *London Review of Education,* 5(2) *July Special Issue on Wisdom,* 143–158.

Thomson, P. (2002). *Schooling the rustbelt kids: Making the difference in changing times.* Crows Nest: Allen & Unwin.

Thomson, P. and Hall, C. (2008). Opportunities missed and/or thwarted? 'Funds of knowledge' meet the English national curriculum. *The Curriculum Journal,* 19(2), 87–103.

Tizard, B. and Hughes, M. (1984). *Young children learning talking and thinking at home and at school.* London: Fontana.

Torrance, H. and Pryor, J. (1998). *Investigating formative assessment.* Buckingham: Open University Press.

Vandenbroeck, M. and Bouverne-De Bie, M. (2006). Children's agency and educational norms: A tensed negotiation. *Childhood,* 13(1), 127–143.

Vandenbroeck, M., Roets, G. and Snoeck, A. (2009). Immigrant mothers crossing borders: Nomadic identities and multiple belongings in early childhood education. *European Early Childhood Education Research Journal,* 17(2), 203–16.

Walker, D. and Nocon, H. (2007). Boundary-crossing competence: Theoretical considerations and educational design. *Mind, Culture, and Activity,* 14(3), 178–95.

Walsh, F. (1998). *Strengthening family resilience.* New York: The Guilford Press.

Wells, G. and Claxton, G. (2002). *Learning for life in the 21st century.* Oxford: Blackwell.

Wenger, E. (1998). *Communities of practice: Learning, meaning, and identity.* Cambridge: Cambridge University Press.

Wertsch, J.V. (1991). *Voices of the mind: A sociocultural approach to mediated action.* Cambridge, MA: Harvard University Press.

Wertsch, J.V. (1997). Narrative tools of history and identity. *Culture & Psychology,* 3(1), 5–20.

Wertsch, J.V. (1998). *Mind as action.* New York: Oxford University Press.

Whalley, M. (2001). *Involving parents in their child's learning.* London: Sage.

Wiliam, D., Lee, C., Harrison, C. and Black, P. (2004). Teachers developing assessment for learning: Impact on student achievement. *Assessment in Education: Principles, Policy & Practice,* 11(1), 49–65.

Index

Note: page numbers in *italic* refer to Learning Stories or tables.

978-1-84920-554-2

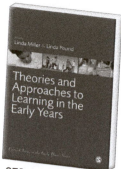

978-1-84920-578-8

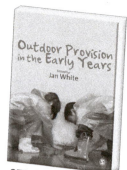

978-1-4129-2309-5

978-1-84920-464-4

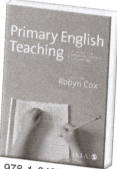

978-1-84920-196-4

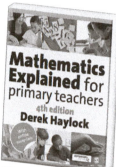

978-1-84860-197-0

978-1-84920-116-2

978-1-84920-520-7

978-1-84860-997-6

Find out more about these titles and our wide range of books for education students and practitioners at **www.sagepub.co.uk/education**

EXCITING EARLY YEARS AND PRIMARY TEXTS FROM SAGE

978-1-84860-616-6

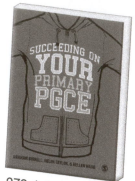

978-1-84920-030-1

978-1-84920-114-8

978-1-84860-713-2

978-1-84920-076-9

978-1-84920-126-1

978-1-84920-078-3

Find out more about these titles and our wide range of books for education students and practitioners at **www.sagepub.co.uk/education**

EXCITING EDUCATION TEXTS FROM SAGE